STEEL CITY
MAFIA

STEEL CITY
MAFIA

BLOOD, BETRAYAL AND PITTSBURGH'S LAST DON

PAUL N. HODOS

THE
History
PRESS

Published by The History Press
Charleston, SC
www.historypress.com

First published 2023

Manufactured in the United States

ISBN 9781467153751

Library of Congress Control Number: 2022949640

To my parents, Paul and Barbara, for instilling a love of history in me; to SO-11, DTOU and PCCRIU for giving me a love of truth based on evidence; and to the Pittsburgh FBI and Cleveland FBI organized crime squads, the IRS, DEA, Pennsylvania State Police, Prosecutor Paul Gains's office, West Virginia and Ohio authorities and the Pennsylvania Crime Commission agents and analysts who combined to destroy the mob.

CONTENTS

ACKNOWLEDGEMENTS

T hank you to former FBI special agent Roger Greenbank for contributing his vital knowledge to this book and for leading the fight against the Pittsburgh mafia for so long. Thanks to true crime author Scott Burnstein for his advice and information. A very special thank-you to JCB1977 for his invaluable help in researching this mob family. He is a true expert.

THE PITTSBURGH FAMILY
CIRCA 1987–1990

*Includes only made members and important associates in charge of major towns.

BOSS: Mike Genovese

UNDERBOSS: Charles "Chucky" Porter, Joseph "Jo Jo" Pecora (died in 1987)

CONSIGLIERE: Charlie Imburgia

LIEUTENANT: Louis Raucci

BOSS'S REPRESENTATIVE: Henry "Zebo" Zottola

CAPOS: Antonio Ripepi, John Bazzano Jr.

GREATER PITTSBURGH AREA MADE MEMBERS: Joe Sica, Frank Amato Jr., Anthony "Wango" Capizzi, Louis Volpe

NEW KENSINGTON MADE MEMBER: Thomas "Sonny" Ciancutti

YOUNGSTOWN MADE MEMBERS: Vincenzo "Two Gun Jimmy" Prato, "Little Joey" Naples, Lenny Strollo

CANTON MADE MEMBER: Pasquale Ferruccio

STEUBENVILLE MADE MEMBER: Jimmy Tripodi

WHEELING ASSOCIATE: Paul "No Legs" Hankish

JOHNSTOWN ASSOCIATES: Mike Gulino and Frederick Piera

ALTOONA MEMBER: John Verilla (in prison from 1984 onward)

ALTOONA ASSOCIATE: Alfred Corbo

CAST OF CHARACTERS

ALTSHULER, BERNARD: Strollo's main lieutenant in the Youngstown crew, died in prison

AMATO, FRANK, JR.: Mob member and son of former boss Frank Amato Sr.

AMATO, FRANK, SR.: Boss of Pittsburgh in the 1940s and 1950s

BATCHO, MARK: Biondillo's bodyguard and a hit man for Strollo

BAZZANO, JOHN, JR.: Mob capo and son of the murdered boss John Bazzano Sr.

BAZZANO, JOHN, SR.: Boss of Pittsburgh in the 1930s, assassinated

BERTONE, JOSEPH: Alleged drug dealer, restaurateur and murder victim

BIONDILLO, ERNEST: Naples's main lieutenant in the Youngstown crew, murdered

BRICKER, ROBERT: Hit man and murderer

CAPIZZI, ANTHONY: Made member

CAPIZZI, VINCENZO: Boss of Pittsburgh in the late 1930s

CARABBIA, CHARLES: Cleveland faction leader and murder victim

CARACCIOLO, VINCENT: Verilla's main enforcer in Altoona, imprisoned for life

CARAMADRE, JOHN: Verilla's main lieutenant in Altoona

CHIARELLI, GENO: Important associate, bank robber and drug middleman

CIANCUTTI, THOMAS: Mob member and head of the New Kensington rackets

CORBO, ALFRED: Mob associate and leader of the Altoona faction after Verilla's imprisonment

DEROSE, JOSEPH, JR.: Cleveland faction hit man and murder victim

DROZNEK, MARVIN: Mob associate under Frank Amato Jr. and a government witness

FERRUCCIO, PASQUALE: Mob member and leading conspirator in the Rincon Casino takeover

GARONO, LAWRENCE: Mob associate and one of Strollo's lieutenants

GENOVESE, MICHAEL: Boss of the Pittsburgh family from December 1984 to October 2006

GESUALE, EUGENE: Mob associate and drug dealer under Porter in the 1970s and 1980s

GIGANTE, VINCENT: Boss of New York's Genovese family

HANKISH, PAUL: Mob associate and leader of the Wheeling crew

IMBURGIA, CHARLES: Longtime consigliere of the Pittsburgh family

LAROCCA, JOHN: Boss of Pittsburgh from 1956 to 1984

LEONETTI, PHILIP: Underboss of the Philadelphia family

LICAVOLI, JAMES: Boss of the Cleveland family

MANCINI, ROBERT: Bookmaker in McKees Rocks and murder victim

MANNARINO, GABRIEL: Underboss to John LaRocca until 1980 and the racket king of New Kensington

MARANO, ALPHONSE: Murdered mob associate

MILANO, PETER: Boss of the Los Angeles family

MONASTERO, STEFANO: Boss of Pittsburgh in the 1920s, assassinated

NAPLES, JOSEPH: Mob member and leader of the Youngstown crew, murdered

PIERA, FREDERICK: Mob associate in Johnstown

PIKE, MELVIN: Hit man and murder victim

PORTER, CHARLES: Underboss of Pittsburgh from 1987 to 1990 and a government informant

PRATO, VINCENZO: Made member and leader of Youngstown crew

PROSDOCIMO, WILLIAM: Leader of a mob-affiliated drug gang in Squirrel Hill and a government witness

RAUCCI, LOUIS: High-ranking member in the 1980s

REGINO, JOSEPH: Capo of Johnstown and Altoona

RIDDLE, JEFFREY: Altshuler's lieutenant, hit man and gambling operative in Mahoning Valley

RIPEPI, ANTONIO: Mob capo and longtime member

ROSA, JOSEPH: Mob associate under Porter and a government witness

SCARFO, NICODEMO: Boss of the Philadelphia family

SICA, JOSEPH: Made member and consigliere for a period in the 1980s

SIRAGUSA, JOSEPH: Boss of Pittsburgh in the early 1930s, assassinated

SISMAN, LAWRENCE: Murder victim and mob associate

STROLLO, LENINE: Mob member and leader of the Youngstown crew after Naples's assassination, government witness

VERILLA, JOHN: Made member and leader of the Altoona crew

VOLPE, LOUIS: Mob member and the last of the infamous Volpe brothers

WILLIAMS, ADOLPH: Mob associate and gambling kingpin

ZOTTOLA, HENRY: Mob member and close advisor to Mike Genovese, lead conspirator in casino takeover

THE ASSASSINATION
OF ALPHONSE MARANO

We have lost a considerable amount of money
due to the carelessness of a few employees.

—*Mike Genovese, alleged acting boss of the Pittsburgh mafia in 1967*[1]

A lphonse Marano was an example of what the FBI described as a "fringe racketeer" in their files on the Pittsburgh mafia family.[2] According to newspapers and the FBI, Marano was a twenty-seven-year-old mafia associate who was originally from East Liberty like so many other younger mob recruits in the area. East Liberty's tough Pittsburgh streets were a fertile training ground for mob wannabes, with part of the Pittsburgh mafia's heavyweights having hailed from that neighborhood in their youth.[3] Marano had repeatedly proven himself loyal to the family after being arrested nineteen times for offenses related to illegal gambling over ten years. Marano does not appear to have given the police any information on his associates after these arrests and was rewarded with steady employment in the mafia's illegal gambling enterprises as a result.[4] Gambling was the bread and butter of the mob across the country, and it was no different in Pittsburgh. Gambling profits are what kept the Cosa Nostra afloat after the windfalls of illegal liquor had disappeared with the end of Prohibition decades earlier.

In 1966 and 1967, Marano was living in Penn Hills and had started to branch out into prostitution. He became the pimp for a group of young prostitutes who worked the East Liberty clubs. He was also listed as the operator of an illegal Pittsburgh gambling den called the Red Eagle Club that had been raided in 1966. Marano was arrested during the raid and charged with keeping a gambling house. The Red Eagle had been raided before when the patrons' wives complained to authorities that their husbands had lost all their money gambling there. Marano was not married and was described by one FBI informant as a slovenly, uncouth and uneducated man with a propensity to buy expensive cars, despite his lack of money. As a result of his alleged carelessness, Marano does not appear to have been on the fast track to becoming a made member of alleged mafia boss John LaRocca's Pittsburgh family, but he was still a fairly competent associate. Marano had just taken a job at a used car lot as a part-time salesman in 1967; this could have been a cover job, giving Marano a way to account for his income with the Internal Revenue Service or whoever else might be investigating him at any given time. The Pittsburgh family had a long record of using hotels, car washes and secondhand car lots as places where their members and associates had no-show jobs.[5]

Marano was last seen by his aunt on the afternoon of Wednesday, December 13, 1967. He had also been seen by his supervisor at the used car lot a few days before. Marano was described by police as wearing "sports clothing" on December 13 and the next day. The term conjures up cliché images of young gangsters wearing dark track suits; although what that type of outfit would have looked like in 1967 is a little hard to piece together, given that this particular mafia cliché was born in the 1980s and 1990s.

At 8:45 a.m. on Thursday, December 14, 1967, Louis Capretto of Yukon, Pennsylvania, was driving on a desolate stretch of rural blacktop road between his hometown and Waltz Mills, right off Interstate 70 near Mount Pleasant, Pennsylvania. As Louis was driving to get a tire repaired, he noted a car parked on the side of the road; part of the car was on the blacktop, and the rest was off the road's surface. According to police, Louis inspected the scene further and saw the dead body of Marano slumped over on the passenger side of the car with three bullet wounds on the left side of his head. He was shot by a person on the driver side. The window to the right of his head was shattered and covered in blood. The weapon was determined by the police to be a .38-caliber revolver, but it was never found. The state police searched the car for fingerprints but failed to find any of use to the case.

Marano's simple life of crime at the edges of Pittsburgh's Cosa Nostra started to unravel a year and a half before his murder when he inadvertently befriended an undercover IRS agent who was investigating the Pittsburgh family's interests in illegal gambling. Marano and others had accepted the agent into their confidences, invited him to their homes and, worst of all, introduced him to other members and associates of the mob. The Pennsylvania Crime Commission's 1970 report stated that Marano had worked in the gambling and prostitution ring of Pittsburgh family racketeer Augustine Ferrone and his two associates, Paul Scolieri and Anthony Capizzi. Marano's friendship with the undercover agent compromised Ferrone's operation and led to Ferrone's and his associates' arrest.[6] Marano had innocently put the family's core moneymaker, gambling, at risk of disruption from law enforcement. A few weeks before Marano's untimely death, the family found out that the individual in question was a federal agent after the FBI and IRS raided two extremely lucrative illegal gambling establishments named the Lantern Inn in New Cumberland, West Virginia, and the Red Dog in Chester, West Virginia, on November 5, 1967. The raids were carried out based on information from the undercover agent.

According to multiple FBI informants, Mike Genovese was angry and out for blood after the raids. The temporary head of the Pittsburgh mafia and heir apparent to John LaRocca's criminal empire was the acting boss of the family in December 1967, since LaRocca was taking his customary monthslong vacation down in Florida to escape the brutal western Pennsylvania winters. Genovese, known as a Pittsburgh homebody who rarely left the area, was usually the boss in training during the winter months into the 1970s. Informants stated that when Genovese was in charge, he always stirred the pot and that everyone feared crossing him while LaRocca was gone. The gangsters felt relieved when the old man returned from Florida to take the reins back in the spring. Genovese and the family had lost a lot of money due to the raid on the West Virginia gambling joints. According to the same FBI informants, Genovese wanted to find out who had introduced this early version of Donnie Brasco to his family and pushed the mafia's business out into the limelight. Genovese, more than anything else, hated publicity, and when there were headlines about Cosa Nostra business, he would sometimes disappear for days and refuse to speak to anyone about the rackets. The newspapers enraged Genovese, who was otherwise known for his calm and cool demeanor.[7]

On the night of December 11, 1967, Genovese reportedly entered the Aloysius Club in Pittsburgh. The club was an after-hours joint controlled by the family that also served as a place to earn legitimate income for the aforementioned "fringe racketeers" whom the mafia relied on to do the dirty work of the organization. Genovese immediately ordered that the club be closed and all the patrons thrown out. After the place was cleared, he closely questioned each employee individually in front of the group at a big table in the club about their relationship or lack thereof with the undercover IRS agent. Marano had many jobs, and one of those was as a doorman for the clubs in West Virginia. He was also the current bartender of the Aloysius Club. Genovese, according to an FBI informant, questioned Marano very closely after he realized that Marano had introduced the agent to other people in the family.

On December 12, according to an FBI informant, Genovese came back to the club and cleared it to gather all the employees at the big table for a second time. This time, he focused in on Marano immediately and told him that he found out that what Marano had said to him the night before was a lie and that, in truth, Marano had been close to the undercover agent. Genovese then dismissed Marano from the table and stared at the other employees in silence for what must have seemed like an excruciatingly awkward amount of time before closing his hand into a fist and pointing his thumb down like a Roman emperor condemning a defeated gladiator to death in the Colosseum. He then turned and walked away.[8]

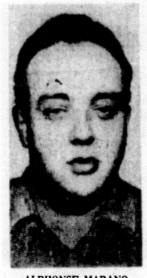

ALPHONSE MARANO
Shot three times.

Gangster-Style Slaying Probed

Penn Hills Man Shot In Westmoreland

Alphonse Marano. *As printed in the* Pittsburgh Post-Gazette.

FBI informants reporting on the murder alleged either Genovese or LaRocca had given the order to kill Marano and transmitted the contract through an unknown third person who then hired the killer or killers. One informant stated that Marano's friends had committed the homicide. This is a well-known mafia tactic to lull the victim into a false sense of security while they are taken on a ride from which they will never return. The murder caused the Pittsburgh Police Department to station officers outside of all the known illegal gambling joints in their jurisdiction from December 18 to January 1 to send a message that further bloodshed would not be tolerated. The murder likely cost the family even more revenue as a result. Security was also increased at the illegal gambling dens owned by the Borgata. Genovese also increased his personal security after Marano's death and forbid anyone to conduct business at his residence on a farm in West Deer, Pennsylvania. All contacts between Genovese and his underlings had to be arranged through Genovese's brother Phil for a time.[9]

FBI informants later alleged that the murder was meant to be a message to all the family's members and associates to be more careful when they took people into their confidences and introduced them to the family. Genovese reportedly meant for the killing to force people to do some background checks on new faces rather than just accept them without asking any questions. Marano is a tragic and sad figure in some respects, as his only legacy was to be used to teach a lesson to the rest of his mafia associates about what would happen if they were not careful. The homicide of Marano, like many other organized crime–related murders in Pittsburgh, was never solved, and no one was prosecuted for the murder of the young man.[10]

Mike Genovese had allegedly made his point, and the lower-level racketeers were reportedly so fearful that they did not dare speak Marano's name or talk about anything related to the incident. As the years rolled through the 1970s and early 1980s, Genovese built on his reputation for secrecy and ruthlessness until LaRocca finally died and Genovese ascended to the top of a mafia family that was on the verge of both great power and a great fall. Genovese was there to witness and lead the Borgata through it all, and the Marano affair would seem minor compared to the tempests to come.

1

FRIENDS PAST
AND FAMILY PLANNING

Michael Genovese, at some point, gets a portion of everything.[11]

—alleged statement of a Pittsburgh mafia member

AMATO'S LEGACY AND THE BIRTH
OF THE STEEL CITY MAFIA

Frank Amato Sr. was the first boss who solidified Cosa Nostra's control of the fractured and ethnically diverse Italian underworld in the Pittsburgh area and banished the infighting that had plagued his predecessors' too-short reigns. The Italian community in Pittsburgh in the first half of the twentieth century was thriving in neighborhoods like Bloomfield, East Liberty, Larimer, Hays and even the Hill District, among others. There was a robust Italian population at the time that lost a small percentage of its young men to the rackets rather than the mills and coal mines. The Italian underworld of western Pennsylvania from the late 1800s to the teens and twenties of the last century was a dizzying tornado of factions and figures with no one clearly in charge until the mid-1920s. In addition, the Italians were competing with other ethnic groups and even gangs of police and politicians who were also running illegal booze.[12]

The first identified Cosa Nostra godfather in Pittsburgh, Stefano Monastero, was killed in a hail of shotgun bullets outside a hospital in 1929. He had arrived in his bulletproof car with a second car of bodyguards behind him, but there was a vehicle full of assassins at the location in advance and they got him.[13] In 1931, Joseph Siragusa, Monastero's successor, was gunned down in his home by three men while shaving. His parrot allegedly lamented, "Poor Joe," repeatedly when the police arrived.[14] John Bazzano Sr. became the new boss and tried to cement his rule by assassinating his rivals the Volpe brothers. Bazzano was able to kill three of them in a daring daylight assault on a coffee shop they frequented, but five remained alive and two went to the newly formed Mafia Commission in New York to complain about Bazzano. Bazzano was lured to New York with a dinner that was held in his honor and attended by multiple high-ranking bosses. There, Bazzano was attacked with ice picks and garroted. His body was found in a burlap sack on a street in Brooklyn; his tongue had been cut out and his mouth taped shut.[15] Vincenzo Capizzi succeeded Bazzano but stepped down after only a few years. Between 1926 and 1933, there were more than two hundred organized crime–related murders in Pittsburgh during the chaos of Prohibition.[16]

Amato's time on the throne was relatively peaceful, and the mob was able to get out of the headlines and back to making money. Amato had the top spot from 1937 to 1956, when he stepped down due to a kidney problem. Amato remained active in the mob for many more years as an advisor to the next boss until he died in 1973. The manner in which the Pittsburgh family was able to change dons and even allow their leader to retire without bloodshed after 1937 was quite frankly amazing and shows that the Borgata had a very well-controlled hierarchy at the time that was genuinely reluctant to murder actual Cosa Nostra members. Associates, unfortunately for them, were a little more disposable to the made guys and were not infrequently killed.[17]

Opposite, top: Joseph Siragusa. *Courtesy of the* Pittsburgh Post-Gazette.

Opposite, middle: John Bazzano Sr. *Courtesy of the* Pittsburgh Post-Gazette.

Opposite, bottom: Frank Amato Sr. *Courtesy of the* Pittsburgh Post-Gazette.

Left: John Bazzano Sr.'s casket being carried from his home. *Courtesy of the* Pittsburgh Post-Gazette.

Amato's successor had worked with the old man and the New Kensington faction of the family for years in the pinball, jukebox and illegal gambling business. John Sebastian LaRocca took over the family and almost immediately made it known that his successor would be Mike Genovese. LaRocca had worked with Genovese in the mob front LaRocca and Genovese Amusements in the 1950s and took a liking to his low-key and secretive style. This author also suspects, although there is only circumstantial evidence, that LaRocca was trying to mollify the younger generation of mafia associates in the East Liberty/Larimer area by anointing their highly respected leader as the next godfather. According to FBI informants, LaRocca and Genovese were always keen to keep the young toughs from Genovese's old neighborhood busy with legitimate employment as well as the rackets. The kids from Larimer were often working the menial jobs at Genovese's Archie's Automatic Carwash or LaRocca's Allegheny Car Wash. LaRocca also had interests in the alleged mob front Keystone Sales Company in Johnstown. LaRocca, like Amato before him, did not seek the spotlight—although, he was widely respected throughout the underworld and even the legitimate world's business community. Under his reign, the family had members in areas as distant as Rochester, New York, and San Jose, California. LaRocca also had friends

Top, left: John LaRocca was a nationally known crime figure who earned respect across the United States at the height of the mafia's power before the RICO law. *Courtesy of the Pittsburgh Post-Gazette.*

Top, right: Keystone Sales Company. *Courtesy of the Pennsylvania State Archives.*

Bottom: Allegheny Car Wash. *Courtesy of the Pennsylvania State Archives.*

Left: Antonio Ripepi was a longtime member and capo. *Courtesy of the Pennsylvania State Archives.*

Right: Frank Sinatra (*second from right*) and alleged made man "Wango" Capizzi (*far right*). *Courtesy of an anonymous researcher.*

from Florida to New York and beyond. However, those connections would weaken as the old bosses either grew old, died or were imprisoned.

The Pittsburgh mob of LaRocca and Genovese was both a hierarchical and decentralized organization, with crews and territory bosses spread out in local towns like Youngstown, Altoona, Johnstown, Erie, Wheeling and Steubenville. For example, Steubenville was run for decades by alleged made members James Tripodi and Cosmo Quattrone. They were already in their eighties when most of the characters in this story came into their own.[18]

LaRocca and his secretive family also allowed themselves some brushes with celebrity. This included Genovese and LaRocca's friendship with Frank Sinatra, who came to a party at made man Antonio Ripepi's house in 1967, and the family's allegedly friendly relationship with Dean Martin.

THE BOSS'S ROLE AND THE NEW YORK FACTOR

In Cosa Nostra, the boss's word is law, and with LaRocca, things were no different. He had the power of life and death over his members and associates at all times. He also had the authority to accept or reject the schemes and scams his underlings came up with. He could negotiate with other families and compel actions on the part of his Borgata under pain of death. However, he wasn't all-powerful. The smaller families who were in New York's long shadow seemingly answered to the commission. The commission was a ruling panel that oversaw the mob's affairs and was mostly composed of the five mafia families of New York. Pittsburgh was represented on the commission by the powerful Genovese family of New York. Phil Leonetti, Nicodemo Scarfo's underboss in the Philadelphia mob family, stated that the Genovese family also represented Philadelphia on the commission during Scarfo's reign. The Genovese family interfered in Philly's affairs for strategic decisions, like the choice of a new boss. Nicky Scarfo got approval from Genovese boss Vincent Gigante before he ascended to power in his own family.[19]

There are tantalizing clues that a similar arrangement may have been in place in Pittsburgh. Samuel "the Plumber" DeCavalcante, head of the North Jersey mob, stated on a wiretap that LaRocca had been placed "on the shelf" while the commission took charge of the Pittsburgh family when he first became the boss. LaRocca took orders from them until they were satisfied that he was boss material. The family reverted to his control shortly thereafter. The commission could exercise such control in those days because the Cosa Nostra was very rule and tradition bound, and many bosses believed in the power of those rules. Also, on a more practical level, the five families of New York had hundreds of made members between them and could destroy any of the smaller families' administrations if they stepped out of line, like they had when Bazzano made his move against the Volpes.

In addition, in an FBI informant report, the informant describes that LaRocca will need to answer to his "superiors" for a situation involving an underling going to prison because an important Pittsburgh gambling figure had potentially informed on him.[20] The relationship between the small family bosses and the commission is still shrouded in secrecy and was likely known only by those in the hierarchy of the family.

According to a high-level government witness, as quoted in the book *Mob Boss*, the Pittsburgh family was small by design for secrecy reasons and the hierarchy preferred that new family members and associates had connections to blood family members who had already been inducted into the Borgata. The witness confirmed that the Pittsburgh family was connected to New York's secretive Genovese family but that even Vincent Gigante's group didn't have control over who Pittsburgh inducted. The family decided which people they wanted to make. The government witness stated that if the Pittsburgh family made a mistake with who they let into their close-knit group, which he described as being similar to a village in Sicily or Calabria, they would simply take the guy "out to the Monongahela River, and that was the end of it."[21] However, according to an interviewed source who wishes to remain anonymous, the Genovese family did dictate *when* Pittsburgh could induct new members, even if *who* they inducted was up to Pittsburgh. The Genovese family in New York had advised that Pittsburgh could replace only those members who had died, so the family could never grow any larger.

THE BOSS'S BEGINNINGS AND FAMILY LIFE

On April 9, 1919, Michael James Genovese was born to Italian immigrants Tony and Ursula Genovese of the Italian Larimer neighborhood of Pittsburgh at their home on 313 Larimer Avenue.[22] Genovese's parents were from a town outside of Naples called Roccarainola. Genovese had two brothers; Felix was his older brother and Fiore the younger. He also had three sisters. No connection to the rackets is evident in the boy's parents, except for an arrest of his mother for moonshine production in the 1930s. However, the family was apparently not troubled by Mike's affiliation with organized crime, since his father would visit his son's Larimer bar and illegal gambling establishment called the Genovese Cocktail Lounge and later the Red Eagle Club in the 1950s.[23] There were also reports that Genovese ran numbers out of his family's house early in his career.[24]

According to the FBI, Genovese only made it to the ninth grade before dropping out of school in 1934 to attend a trade school. It is not clear if he ever actually attended the trade school. His IQ score was listed as a low 77; although, Genovese would show that this score was not representative of his superb intellect. His older brother, Felix, also known as Phil, was apparently in the Pittsburgh mob before Mike but was not considered leadership material due to his violent temper, overindulgence in scotch and blatant philandering. Felix's bad tendencies were supplemented by numerous arrests. He just wasn't as careful as Mike. Fiore, the younger brother, was considered less than serious by his mob colleagues, despite being a trusted associate.

In March 1971, tragedy struck Genovese's family when Fiore was walking out of an office in Larimer with another man. Suddenly, Nicholas Gelormini, an allegedly mentally handicapped man who worked at the Red Eagle Club, shot at him with a .32-caliber handgun from a car. The shots missed, so Gelormini hopped out and finished Fiore off. Gelormini then got into a shootout with police before he was apprehended. Gelormini was looking for vengeance on the mobsters who teased him at work.

Genovese (*right*) holding court at the Red Eagle Bar. *Courtesy of an anonymous researcher.*

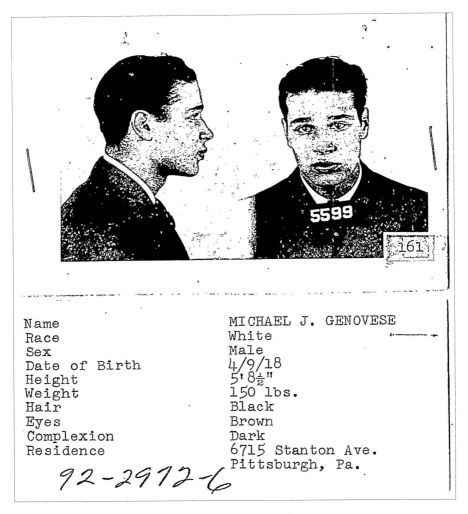

```
5599
161
```

Name	MICHAEL J. GENOVESE
Race	White
Sex	Male
Date of Birth	4/9/18
Height	5'8½"
Weight	150 lbs.
Hair	Black
Eyes	Brown
Complexion	Dark
Residence	6715 Stanton Ave. Pittsburgh, Pa.

92-2972-6

A teenaged mug shot of Michael Genovese. *FBI photograph.*

He had tried to kill his main tormentor, mob associate Eugene Gesuale, earlier, but Gesuale wouldn't come out of his house so Gelormini decided to kill someone else. According to FBI informants, Genovese wanted to kill Gelormini but was persuaded by his mentor and boss John LaRocca to let it go since Gelormini was described as "insane" and the killing was not related to business.[25]

Genovese's first known brush with the law occurred in September 1936, when he and another teenager punched a young man and robbed him of a few dollars on Larimer Avenue. Genovese's victim was a good sketch artist and drew a picture of his attacker that was used by the police to apprehend Genovese. Genovese was described as a boxer at the time. Genovese's boxing career was short and garnered him no real success, but he was fond of the sport for the rest of his life. Genovese received two years of probation for the robbery and allegedly worked as a marble setter's helper at the Washington Marble Company after receiving his sentence. In 1945, he had another run-in with the law when he was arrested in Youngstown, Ohio, for carrying a loaded .32-caliber revolver and a blackjack while "walking suspiciously." The charge was tossed after Genovese pleaded not guilty. Numbers writers who knew Genovese at the time stated he was a "young, fresh kid" trying to break into organized crime. Genovese reportedly concocted a plan to get arrested so he would not be drafted and sent off to fight in World War II. The plan appears to have worked, as he never served in the military.[26]

Genovese's personal life was pretty standard for a mobster and was a little chaotic at times. He was married in 1939 but became separated from his first wife when he allegedly cheated on her. He had two daughters in his first marriage. He later married a woman who already had a daughter and then adopted a son with his second wife. His first wife claimed to the FBI that Genovese didn't keep up with his child support payments, but it appears he kept in touch with his daughters after they moved out to California. In 1956, Genovese and his second wife moved to a converted chicken farm on eighty-two acres of land in rural Gibsonia, Pennsylvania, close to West Deer on curvy Clendenning Road. Genovese and the owner of the farm claimed that Genovese lived there rent free since he helped run the farm and hired contractors to improve the buildings. However, FBI informants stated that the farm's owner, an Italian man from East Liberty, was indebted to Genovese for gambling losses and had to give the farm up to pay the rising gangster back. The farm was a modest home for a relatively modest mobster whose only flashy tendency was buying a Cadillac to drive around in.

The property contained a frame house, wagon shed, garage, frame barn, three-story chicken house and a two-story frame brick house.[27] Genovese lived at the farm for decades and particularly enjoyed mowing the big lawn on a tractor and taking care of the horses he kept there. He also had "police dogs" roaming the property to keep the place secure. It was a peaceful retreat that rarely hosted mafia business meetings—except an occasional hunting trip or barbeque on the property with the guys. Genovese loved the western Pennsylvania hunting tradition and was a local boy at heart. He kept the acreage intact the entire time he lived there, as he did not want any close

Mike Genovese on his horse at his farm. *Courtesy of an anonymous researcher.*

neighbors or developers coming into the area. The farm and its buildings grew in size as time went on, but the original farm was quite modest, with a small, simple house and a few rooms that Genovese called home. Informants reported Genovese had two .22 pistols in a heavily ornamented gun belt that evoked an Old West style hanging just inside the door. The interior of the house was described as being designed with "early American" décor.

Genovese's second wife died in 1998, and the boss was so secretive at that point that he omitted his name from the obituary. He was married a third time in the first decade of the 2000s to a longtime girlfriend who described him as living paycheck to paycheck. She said he was a good, classy and very proud man who would "keep things to himself." She also stated he was a meticulous dresser who always had to have what he considered to be a proper appearance.[28]

GENOVESE ASCENDANT

Genovese was described by the FBI as being dangerous with a knife, and he was known as one of the toughest mob guys around, despite his less than imposing appearance. He stood at five feet, eight inches tall and weighed about 160 pounds. He had a short and stocky build, curly black

Left: Gabriel "Kelly" Mannarino. *As printed in the* Pittsburgh Post-Gazette.

Above: Genovese (*top row, second from right, smoking*) and Mannarino (*top row, third from right, next to Genovese*) at a bar. *Courtesy of an anonymous researcher.*

hair, brown eyes and a dark complexion. He had come up as a bodyguard for the powerful Mannarino brothers of New Kensington: Gabriel, also known as "Kelly," and Sam. They ruled New Kensington with an iron grip and a relatively soft hand through their extensive illegal gambling enterprise that was protected by corrupted local officials who answered to the brothers. Kelly Mannarino even had strong connections to organized crime heavy hitter Meyer Lansky.[29] It appears Genovese entered the Pittsburgh crime family's ranks as an associate and later became a made man during Frank Amato Sr.'s reign. Genovese earned most of his money in the early 1950s and previously on horse and baseball betting and had interests in the numbers rackets as well.

Genovese's associates in the underworld stated that he had "clean habits" and was "conservative." He was also known for being cheap and often complained of not having any money. He was infamous as the guy who had the "first nickel he ever earned." FBI agents thought of him as almost excessively polite, and he was always a little nervous when they talked to him. Genovese always reminded them that he couldn't talk business with an agent but was willing to have a friendly conversation. According to multiple sources, he cheated on his wives, partied with his mafia colleagues and hung out at hotels, bars and restaurants at all times of the day and night, but he kept his gambling and fun modest for a gangster and crafted a reputation of being someone who was steady. In a nutshell, he wasn't flashy, overly violent and careless with his words like his future contemporaries in other families, such as John Gotti and Nicodemo Scarfo. Genovese was rarely caught on a wire and only talked to select people about select things. He insulated himself throughout his criminal career due to a few seminal events in his life that occurred between the late 1950s and the mid-1970s.[30]

The first of these events happened just as the mafia and Mike Genovese's fortunes changed forever on November 14, 1957, at mob boss Joseph Barbara's estate in Apalachin, New York. A grand underworld meeting of bosses took place, with over one hundred gangsters in attendance. The meeting was allegedly called to confirm Vito Genovese, no relation to Mike per the FBI, as the boss of one of New York's five families. Mike Genovese told informants that the mobsters discussed and approved of a nationwide plan to use hotels to launder illegal gambling profits. The Pittsburgh family would allegedly build two hotels for this purpose. Genovese's main hotel and sometime headquarters in the 1960s was called the Phoenix and was located in Monroeville.[31]

Apalachin was also a complete fiasco that ended up forcing Director J. Edgar Hoover of the FBI to recognize the mob as a criminal threat. The national strategy meeting showed a level of sophistication in the mafia that was frankly shocking to the public and the government. The New York State Police noticed the large numbers of out-of-state plates traveling into tiny Apalachin and became suspicious, given that a smaller underworld meeting had occurred there only the year before. They figured out some of the people at the Barbara estate were racketeers and started to take down license plate numbers while their cars were parked and at checkpoints leading out of the area. The attendees panicked; some tried to escape in their cars, and others ran into the woods on foot. Genovese and Kelly Mannarino were caught and stopped by police in Mannarino's car. They were with two mobsters from the Bufalino crime family based in Scranton, Pennsylvania. Genovese was interviewed by police after his apprehension and released.[32]

Hoover, despite worries that some of his agents would be corrupted while working the cash-infused mafia, decided to unleash the FBI against the mob after the media firestorm and subsequent government pressure to do something about organized crime post-Apalachin. Genovese soon realized that going to the meeting was a mistake, as the FBI started to surveil him and also interviewed him quite often. The nervous and publicity-shy Genovese hated the fallout, and everybody was feeling the heat in 1958. The bureau opened its first case on Genovese around that time. The first investigation started what would become an effort spanning five decades to try to put Genovese behind federal bars.

Genovese was also served with a subpoena to testify at a federal grand jury to get to the bottom of what was happening at Apalachin. A famous picture of Genovese depicts him testifying and pleading the Fifth Amendment in front of the Senate Labor Rackets Committee; his fingers are in his mouth, and he looks very nervous.[33] Genovese had reason to be nervous, as his questioner, Robert Kennedy, was the brother of the president-elect. Mannarino and LaRocca fled their homes and hid out until

Genovese looks nervous during testimony post-Apalachin. *Courtesy of the Pittsburgh Post-Gazette.*

everything blew over. Mike survived the encounter and became much more secretive than he already was as a result. Once he got back from Apalachin, he immediately sold Archie's Automatic Carwash and shut down the numbers operation he ran out of there. Another media firestorm was already on the way to Genovese by the fall.

In November 1958, a task force of Pennsylvania state troopers, the FBI and the U.S. Border Patrol uncovered a stunning plot that was allegedly headed up by Kelly and Sam Mannarino to ship guns to Fidel Castro's rebels in Cuba to obtain favorable government support for continued mob control of the Sans Souci Casino. This runs counter to the old tale that the mob wanted to keep the old dictator Fulgencio Batista in power because he was beneficial to them. Apparently, he had affected mob profits by interfering with the Sans Souci, and they sought a change in management of the country as a result.

This was an incredibly bold and, in hindsight, stupid move on the Mannarinos' part, since the full weight of state and federal law enforcement was already on the rackets due to the fallout from the Apalachin summit that had just occurred the year before. The state troopers and border patrol agents watched a plane load up with 121 M-1 Garand rifles stolen from a Canton, Ohio armory in October 1958 and a .50-caliber machine gun from an unknown source. The rifles on board did not account for all the rifles that had been stolen in Canton. Law enforcement could not stop the plane from lifting off from the Allegheny Valley Airport, but they did follow and detain the supply truck that had connections to the Mannarino group in New Kensington. The plane was eventually intercepted and followed to a refueling stop at an airport in Morgantown, West Virginia, after authorities attempted to unsuccessfully use military radar stations to track the aircraft.[34] The state troopers also searched Genovese's barn and home for the rest of the rifles but found nothing.

The Borgata survived the Cuba fiasco relatively unscathed, and Genovese became the acting boss of the family for the first time while LaRocca and Mannarino were on the lam in the late 1950s. LaRocca had survived worse. In 1954, the federal government attempted to deport him back to Italy since he had been convicted of larceny, receiving stolen goods and illegal gambling. Pennsylvania's Republican governor John Fine shockingly gave LaRocca a backdated pardon that scuttled the federal government's attempt to banish him.[35] LaRocca's trust in Genovese grew as the 1960s wore on. Genovese would serve as the acting boss for many years to come when LaRocca took his monthslong vacations to Florida with Johnstown capo Joe Regino and both their wives to get away from the harsh Pennsylvania winters at their neighboring summer homes in Pompano Beach.

Genovese's Health and Career Stumbles

On May 13, 1968, Genovese drove up to the Phoenix Motel and lurched out of his car gasping for air and almost falling on the ground when a former used car salesman, whom the mob had reportedly screwed out of his former car business, caught him and summoned a doctor he had been drinking with in the Phoenix Lounge. The former salesman was allowed to sell suits and shoes from the back of his car at the Phoenix and was in the process of doing so when he noticed Genovese in distress. Genovese was taken to Shadyside Hospital, where he had another heart attack while in the lobby. He was placed in the intensive care unit and took months to recover. According to FBI informants, the incident was scary for him personally and exacerbated his already nervous personality, since he now had to worry about dying in addition to his stressful racket duties. The news got out, and some FBI informants thought Genovese was finished as a top leader in Pittsburgh. Genovese's heart would plague him for over a half decade more until he underwent heart surgery that fixed the issue in 1975. After the surgery, he was able to get his physical strength back and reassure LaRocca that he was healthy enough to take over after the old man either died or stepped down.

The vultures were circling, according to FBI informants, but Genovese was able to hold them off by using his brother Felix and friend Joseph Pecora, a future underboss, to help him manage his illegal and legal businesses. Genovese also held the power of life and death over the members and associates of the family while LaRocca was away. Despite his ill health in the late 1960s and early 1970s, Genovese was still greatly feared, and according to an FBI informant, his underlings knew murder was on the table if they disobeyed him. Genovese ordered that his associates should not visit him at the hospital or at his home while he recovered, lest they be identified by law enforcement. As Genovese recovered from his heart surgery in April 1975, his trusted older brother and confidant, Felix, died suddenly. It was a blow that fell just as Genovese was regaining his strength, and it taxed the already overwhelmed mobster even further.

At the same time that Genovese was closing the book on his heart troubles, he was subpoenaed to testify before a grand jury. The federal grand jury sought testimony from Genovese about western Pennsylvania organized crime in return for immunity. Genovese refused to answer the questions and was arrested and placed in prison on April 23, 1974. Genovese was never in prison for a lengthy stay and was perturbed that he did not get any preferential treatment regarding meals, medical checks and movies. Genovese was largely ignored by the prison population.

The small Pittsburgh mafia community was shocked that Genovese could be sent away for not answering questions. Genovese's associates stayed away from the prison for the most part, except to bring Genovese some food from the Phoenix Lounge. Genovese was OK with them keeping their distance, as he did not want law enforcement to use his incarceration as a chance to gather intelligence on the organization. Genovese eventually adapted to life behind bars and the alleged lack of respect given him there. There were only a few Pittsburgh mafia members and associates, and the percentage of the prison population that was connected must have been particularly small at this time. Genovese started to work in the prison's sick bay and as a trainer for the annual Independence Day prison boxing match. Genovese could not resist boxing, and it passed the time.

Tony Grosso, a very successful illegal gambling operator in the Pittsburgh area who was semi-independent from LaRocca's family, had been arrested before Genovese went to prison. Grosso decided to talk to federal authorities about his business and report on corrupt officials he had in his pocket for leniency.

Word in the underworld was that he was talking too much and that Genovese might have been targeted based on Grosso's information. LaRocca was incensed at this, and FBI informants indicated that both Genovese and LaRocca were incredibly angry about the situation. LaRocca pledged to help defend Genovese with the family's funds, and FBI informants noted that LaRocca seemed to be moving to have Grosso killed. The prison Grosso was housed in was susceptible to Cosa Nostra infiltration, according to one informant.

Tony Grosso. *Courtesy of the Pennsylvania State Archives.*

The FBI took the threat so seriously that they approached LaRocca at his headquarters at Allegheny Car Wash out of the blue and warned him that if Grosso was killed, they would immediately look at him as the culprit. LaRocca was amazed that the FBI would be so brazen, but it appears that talk of whacking Grosso died down right after the approach. Grosso had not been touched by the mob in the past because he had a wide network of public officials in his back pocket whom LaRocca's Cosa Nostra family could use when needed, and Grosso provided information to the family about investigations and raids. He provided value to the Cosa Nostra, but compared to the millions he was making from his enterprise, what he gave to LaRocca was paltry.[36] Genovese would have a chance to bite back in the future.

Genovese was allowed to go home on November 27, 1974, after spending about six months in jail, not counting a longer release he had after his initial arrest. The grand jury just faded away after that. He had held his tongue, and the threat posed by the inquiry was gone. Genovese had learned one thing from his experience: he told his associates that he would never go to prison again. It was a promise that would prove to be difficult to keep for a future mob boss, but Mike Genovese would orient his whole career to making it come true.[37]

ALLIES AND MONEY

LaRocca was a well-traveled underworld diplomat, but Genovese had contacts in other families, too. He had friends in Scranton's Bufalino family, Philadelphia's Bruno family, New York's Genovese family, the Detroit family and the Cleveland family. Genovese even had unidentified contacts in Italy. In the 1970s, he instructed Joseph Pecora to contact a list of people, whose names Genovese provided, while Pecora vacationed in Italy.[38] In the mid-1980s, the FBI identified that Genovese called numbers in Spain and Italy, although it was not apparent who the recipients were and it was possible that he was calling blood-related family.[39] Genovese and the family also had contacts in Pittsburgh's Black criminal underworld. In 1968, an informant told the FBI that after riots in Pittsburgh, the Black numbers operators no longer wanted to pay the Cosa Nostra a portion of their profits from the Hill District neighborhood. The only thing that kept the payments coming was the "deep fear" the local operators had of the mob. They allegedly paid $20,000 a day to Mannarino and Genovese at this time.[40] The Pittsburgh family also worked with the Pagans motorcycle gang from time to time.

Genovese was also sophisticated in the manner in which he hid his alleged illegal money. Investing in cash-heavy businesses, like car washes, hotels, nightclubs, restaurants, bars, casinos and real estate, appears to have been standard Pittsburgh mob practice. The FBI suspected Genovese also invested some of his money in apartment buildings in Shadyside, a desirable neighborhood in Pittsburgh. The FBI's suspicions were heightened when they obtained information that Genovese was using a realty company to hide his money.

Victor N. Calautti, a Youngstown, Ohio businessman, was also accused by the FBI of laundering money for several Cosa Nostra heavyweights. Calautti was linked to Pittsburgh mafia member "Little Joey" Naples and Bufalino crime family member William D'Elia, who once allegedly told an informant Calautti was a good person to use to handle mob cash.[41] In 1994, the FBI asserted that Calautti helped Genovese and Russell Bufalino, head of the crime family based in the Pittston/Scranton area, launder their ill-gotten money through English and Swiss bank accounts. Naples, the Pittsburgh mob member, allegedly told an informant that Calautti had been part of a scheme to import $200 million in drug money from Italy to the United States for unnamed investments through Luxembourg. Calautti also allegedly used a bank in Antwerp, Belgium, to move funds. Calautti reportedly stated that he used foreign and offshore accounts to hide the money and avoid taxes. Naples and Calautti collected $700,000 from just one money laundering job. Calautti was also allegedly involved in a scheme with D'Elia to haul trash from New York City to Ohio by utilizing a corrupt Pennsylvania environmental services official.

The amounts and sophistication of the network were stunning and illustrated the connections even small Cosa Nostra families like Pittsburgh could cultivate. The Calautti ring was busted when an undercover FBI agent infiltrated the operations of one of Calautti's associates. The FBI then turned the associate into a cooperating witness.[42]

THE NEW BOSS

According to the Pennsylvania Crime Commission, in the late 1970s, LaRocca started to hand over more and more of his leadership duties to a ruling panel that consisted of Genovese, Pecora and Mannarino. It appears Mannarino, the racket king of New Kensington, officially held the underboss title until he died in 1980. Throughout the 1970s, FBI informants kept saying that Mannarino was angling to unseat Genovese to become the next boss. However, if he was planning to take over, those plans were interrupted by how long old man LaRocca lived and by Mannarino's own death.

After 1980, there were only two possible contenders for the throne. Joseph "Jo Jo" Pecora had been Genovese's go-to guy when he was having heart problems. Pecora also did tasks for Genovese that included driving him around and making sure his family was okay. As stated previously, Pecora became the underboss after Mannarino's death. Genovese was seen as arrogant within the organization and was seemingly more feared than Pecora. In addition, Genovese was a confident and experienced leader who commanded respect by his mere presence. However, Pecora was more popular due to his affable personality and may have been LaRocca's late-in-life favorite over his longtime protégé Genovese.

Pecora was the king of gambling in the West Virginia panhandle and ruled there with a smile rather than an iron fist. He had several gambling joints that had become popular places for Pittsburgh residents to gamble out of state. Pecora had the local officials in his pocket and openly hobnobbed with them. In 1979, all of that came crashing down when the federal government set up a sting operation using a sheriff that a Pecora associate and bookmaker, Silvio "Birdie" Pinciaro, had attempted to bribe with $100,000 a year and the services of a prostitute. The sheriff reported the attempted corruption and then played along while gathering evidence against the gangsters. The sheriff did not think Pecora was boss material and implied he was not smart enough. The case resulted in Pecora serving three years in prison and then probation, which effectively took him out of the running for the boss position.[43]

Right: Jo Jo Pecora. *Courtesy of an anonymous researcher.*

Below: LaRocca (*right*) speaks with alleged member "Wango" Capizzi (*left*) at Allegheny Car Wash just before LaRocca's death. *Courtesy of the Pennsylvania State Archives.*

At the same time Pecora was on probation, John Sebastian LaRocca, the ruler of the Pittsburgh rackets for almost thirty years, died in his bed at his home in Ingomar, Pennsylvania, of congestive heart failure on December 3, 1984. LaRocca's funeral was covered by two newspapers and three TV stations. The mob bodyguards who were trying to keep the funeral a private affair did not appreciate all the attention from the media. One *Pittsburgh Post-Gazette* photographer snapped a photograph of LaRocca's casket as it was carried out of the St. Alexis Church in McCandless, Pennsylvania. Several burly men appeared and menaced the photographer. One of them grabbed his camera and told him, "You better let go of the camera, or I'll break your hand." The photographer let the camera go. The camera was returned to him later without its film. Other media members were also threatened and chased away.[44]

As the media and state law enforcement in Pittsburgh breathlessly reported

Genovese exits the Holiday House just before becoming the new boss in the fall of 1984. *Courtesy of the Pennsylvania State Archives.*

that Pecora would be the next boss, the capos of the Pittsburgh family, Antonio Ripepi, Joseph Regino, John Bazzano Jr. and Mike Genovese, met to vote about a week after LaRocca's death. The assembled leadership selected Michael James Genovese as the next boss.[45] Genovese had waited almost thirty years for this moment. The family he took command of never exceeded twenty made members, with each member having some trusted associates. As fictional Don Carmine Lupertazzi states about his New Jersey counterparts on the hit HBO show *The Sopranos*, the New York families might remark that Pittsburgh was a "glorified crew."[46] However, their profits, activities, influence and reach and the huge size of their territory were far beyond what an average crew in New York City was accustomed to.

Genovese had been schooled well by LaRocca and now finally had the top spot. He would keep himself insulated from the crimes his family committed by using trusted intermediaries to stay in the shadows as much as he could, just like LaRocca had.

However, Genovese also had big plans for the family that was described by the Pennsylvania Crime Commission as aging and slow with a respect problem in the local underworld. LaRocca had not even made any new guys in years. Genovese would change that and make the Pittsburgh mob the dominant criminal force in the region once again.

Resurgence

Genovese's first step in 1986 was to take over the extensive gambling operation of Tony Grosso, who had been indicted and convicted yet again and would likely not see the outside of a prison for years. Genovese had not been fond of Grosso ever since he suspected that he had talked about him to authorities in 1974, during his troubles with the grand jury that sent him to prison. The Grosso operation allegedly netted $30 million a year with over six thousand numbers operators, and that amount was parceled out by the family to gambling associates and brothers Salvatore, Eugene and Junior Williams, as well as Robert Iannelli. Grosso's operation had been the proverbial goose that laid the golden egg that was always just out of the mob's reach due to Grosso's pull with the local politicians. Genovese's decisive move against Grosso and his demand for a higher percentage of the take from Grosso's old operation would allow the family to earn much more from their illegal gambling enterprises than ever before. In addition, the aggressive moves by the family against even smalltime independent gambling operators would add a bonus to the profits from Grosso's old operation.[47]

LaRocca's edict against drug dealing by family members, a relic by the 1970s, would also be lifted. According to the Pennsylvania Crime Commission, one family associate responded that Genovese was "like a breath of fresh air" when it came to his acceptance of drug money. LaRocca had unofficially profited off of drugs, too, and the family started to get into the business through a multitude of associates in the late 1970s as LaRocca's grip loosened. An FBI cooperating witness once detailed in court that the old-school gangsters like Mannarino and LaRocca were against dealing drugs but that everything changed when "Mr. Genovese took over."[48] Members and associates seemingly no longer had to hide their drug deals from the boss.

The street tax on gambling was supplemented by a street tax on drug dealing. Norman Farber, a drug dealer formerly outside of the mafia's control, testified in court that things changed for him when Genovese became the boss. Geno Chiarelli, one of the family's associates, told Farber there was a new "old man" after LaRocca's death and that he was going to "rule the city with an iron fist." Chiarelli demanded a tax of 15 percent of Farber's profits for the right to continue to operate his drug business. Farber lied and said he was out of the business. Chiarelli asked Farber to have a "sit down" with him. Farber foolishly stated, "I'm not going to sit down with any greaseballs." Later, Farber and his girlfriend were walking down the street when they were detained by three armed men and Farber was beat up. His jewelry was stolen and the $11,000 he had in drug profits was taken. Farber was told to never refer to Chiarelli or the "old man" as "greaseballs" again. Farber was also informed that he would be paying a cut of all his profits to the mob from now on. As a sign of good faith, his jewelry was returned to him by Chiarelli.[49]

Genovese made at least four and possibly five new members in the second half of the 1980s to replace those who were aging or had died. The new guys were very active, in some cases well into the 1990s and beyond. Joey Naples, Lenny Strollo, Charles Porter and Sonny Ciancutti rejuvenated the family.[50] Henry "Zebo" Zottola has been variously described by different sources as either a made guy or a powerful associate who was treated as a made man. Genovese had tried to make new members earlier, but New York's Genovese family did not allow him to open up the books in 1985 and he had to wait a year.

Geno Chiarelli. *Courtesy of the Pittsburgh Post-Gazette.*

Genovese's all-encompassing gambling street tax, the new underboss's arbitrarily enforced drug dealing tax, direct dealing in drugs and the newly made members immediately resuscitated the underworld reputation of the Pittsburgh Cosa Nostra. The family was rich, powerful and respected by the criminal element in the area again. Suddenly, the mob was back, and if you wanted to do illegal business in western Pennsylvania, eastern Ohio and West Virginia, you better be ready to pay them. However, the aggressive moves of the early 1980s, as LaRocca's star waned, caught the attention of law enforcement, and that attention would only increase as Genovese's family delved ever deeper into the drug trade.

THE NEW REGIME

The man who collected the various streams of drug trafficking and gambling revenue and funneled it up to the boss was the eventual underboss and right-hand man of Genovese, Charles Porter. Porter was the driving force behind the mob's push into narcotics and was Genovese's choice to take the family into the future, possibly even as Genovese's eventual successor.[51] Later in life, Porter would claim that Genovese actually hated drug dealing but tolerated the trade because Porter made him a lot of money from it. Porter's claim means that, at the very least, Genovese was allowing his guys to be in the drug business and turning a blind eye to where the cash Porter handed him came from.[52]

Porter was also a close associate of LaRocca and appeared at the Allegheny Car Wash multiple times near the end of the old don's life. However, it was Genovese who elevated him to the top of the mob hierarchy. Porter was from Etna, on the high school rifle team and was in the U.S. Army for a few years stationed in Germany. According to a Pittsburgh newspaper, Porter started his criminal life as a "thug who committed strong arm robberies." Porter was said to be the type of guy who would pull a shotgun out at a card game if he thought he was being cheated and once beat a man with a baseball bat to collect on a sports bet.[53] Porter was also a former mailman and a drug trafficker and was prone to getting into fights at bars. As a mafia associate under Kelly Mannarino, he quickly gained a reputation of being an earner and a tough guy who also had the ability to engage in polite diplomacy with other gangsters. According to government witnesses, Porter also ran mob-connected dice games in East Liberty clubs. FBI agents found him to be a gentleman in their presence.[54]

The fifty-two-year-old Porter was inducted into the crime family fairly late in life in 1986 and was almost immediately promoted to underboss but was not of full Italian blood. His Italian heritage came through his mother and his half Italian–half Irish father, which would have precluded him from becoming a member in some other families. The Pittsburgh family was not as strict when it came to this rule, and more than a few talented associates

Left: Charles Porter (*right*) and Eugene Gesuale (*left*) exit the Beacon Club in Squirrel Hill. *FBI photograph*.

Right: Joe Sica. *Courtesy of the Pennsylvania State Archives*.

with only partial or even no Italian blood were treated like members by Genovese and Porter.[55] According to former FBI agent Roger Greenbank, Little Al D'Arco, the former acting boss of New York's Lucchese family and a government witness, stated "that's how they did things down there" in the Pittsburgh family. D'Arco was related to Pittsburgh member Joseph Sica and had a close friendship with him that involved D'Arco traveling to Pittsburgh often. D'Arco even claimed that the Pittsburgh gangsters offered him an ownership stake in their hangout at the Holiday House.[56] D'Arco had helped Sica while he was on the lam in the 1970s, and Sica offered to make him into the Pittsburgh family. D'Arco declined but maintained close ties.

D'Arco also stated he had been tasked to reach out to Pittsburgh to get a bomb to carry out a hit on John Gotti in retaliation for Gotti's unsanctioned killing of former Gambino family boss Paul Castellano. According to D'Arco, the New Yorkers were aware that the Pittsburgh family had experience with explosives and that Sica allegedly had someone on deck to help with Gotti's demise, but the request was canceled after a member of Gotti's hierarchy was killed instead and the matter was dropped.[57]

According to the FBI, Porter met with Genovese at LA Motors in Verona, Pennsylvania, almost every day in the late 1980s.[58] Porter was said to sit on the right-hand side of the don and even represented Genovese at a meeting with another boss. In September 1986, Porter and made member Louis Volpe met with infamous Philadelphia family godfather Nicodemo Scarfo and his underboss Phil Leonetti at the Gambit's Lounge inside a Marriott hotel in Monroeville. The issue that precipitated the meeting was created by the street tax the Pittsburgh family had started to collect on all bookmakers on their turf. The family had attempted to squeeze Joseph Nistico of Clairton, Scarfo's brother-in-law, for a piece of his action, and Nistico had complained to Scarfo. According to Leonetti, Porter bragged at the meeting that he handled many things for Genovese, which included shaking down drug dealers and illegal gambling operators. This incident also shows how secretive Genovese was, since he did not even come out to meet a fellow don who had traveled to his territory for an important meeting.[59] According to former FBI agent Roger Greenbank, the Pittsburgh FBI followed Porter at 7:00 a.m. the day after the Scarfo meeting as he met Genovese in a hardware store parking lot off business Route 22, where they walked and talked for a while.[60] Genovese's caution when it came to Scarfo was rewarded, since shortly after the meeting, Scarfo's regime in Philadelphia imploded and Leonetti eventually became a government witness.

Porter also handled interfamily payments and business. In 1987, right after the death of Pecora, Porter met a Pittsburgh-based ethnic Chinese gambler in Florida to collect a few thousand dollars from a Chinese gambling syndicate that had branches in Chicago, New York and Pittsburgh. LaRocca and Pecora had assisted with a dispute the Chinese had with the Chicago mafia family that had caused their gambling establishment to be shut down. Porter informed the Chinese gambling figure that Porter had taken over Pecora's duties as underboss.[61]

The man right under Porter and named as a lieutenant of the crime family who was said to sit on the left side of Genovese was Louis Raucci. Raucci and Porter both met with Genovese on a daily basis in the 1980s. Raucci was also

Charles Porter. *Courtesy of the Pennsylvania State Archives.*

in charge of the gambling and drug trafficking operations of the family. Raucci made it into the papers in the 1950s as a participant in a dispute over the numbers business in East Liberty. He allegedly bombed two rival establishments and was described as a gunman and a safecracker.[62] Raucci had even gotten into an hour-long shootout with the police that saw him and an accomplice rousted out of their hideout with tear gas in 1953.[63] Raucci also reportedly stole $41,000 from a bank messenger and kidnapped both the messenger and the police escort before getting away with the money in 1959. Raucci was also implicated in a 1970s baby selling scam, in which he and another man and woman allegedly sold babies to desperate would-be parents for thousands of dollars. However, they didn't deliver the babies, so the scheme was actually just an exercise in fraud rather than actual baby trafficking.[64]

Until 1987, when he died, the aforementioned Joseph Pecora was the official underboss. However, the real powerhouses in Genovese's family and the true lieutenants of Genovese were always Raucci and Porter, with Pecora's title a sign of the respect given to the trusted longtime advisor, despite his limited duties in the mid-1980s. Pecora still collected various revenue streams for Genovese before he died when Porter took over that responsibility.[65]

Louis Raucci. *Courtesy of the Pennsylvania State Archives.*

Secretive Eastern Ohio resident Charles Imburgia was reportedly the quiet consigliere of the family after Joe Sica stepped down.[66] Imburgia is mentioned as being loosely involved with a bingo and strip-ticket skimming operation, and the Pennsylvania Crime Commission described him as a "top associate" of Michael Genovese in 1990.[67]

HOLDING COURT

Genovese changed the mob's headquarters from LaRocca's low-key Allegheny Car Wash to the flashier nightclub and hotel named the Holiday House. Genovese, Porter and Raucci held court in the Holiday House in the 1980s until the place closed and burned down in 1988.[68] The Holiday House was a Monroeville landmark and had some of the best acts in town. Big stars and bands, like Frank Sinatra, Frankie Avalon, Tony Bennett, Milton Berle and the Temptations, played at the nine-hundred-seat theater. According to court testimony, Genovese, Porter and Raucci talked with dozens of associates and sometimes accepted packages from them while sitting at a table in the club. The conversations were always whispered, according to law enforcement, and it was difficult to hear what was being discussed. The FBI asserted that Genovese and his associates ran gambling, narcotics trafficking and loansharking operations from their table at the Holiday House, although the FBI was never able to prove conclusively that the mobsters had an ownership stake in the place itself.[69] According to a former FBI agent,

Top: The Holiday House. *Bottom*: The Holiday House's interior. *Author's collection.*

the mobsters also took their girlfriends there for dates and were suspected of using the hotel rooms often for meetings, exchanging stolen property, committing potential sex crimes and making drug deals.[70] In October 1981, Porter married his wife at the Holiday House.

Genovese's next move was to take a page from LaRocca's book. He transferred to a low-key headquarters after the closing of the Holiday House and after his family had been hit with more than a few drug-related prosecutions that involved some of the Borgata's associates. According to FBI files, Genovese owned a gas station directly across from a small restaurant in Verona, Pennsylvania, a suburb of Pittsburgh, which he turned into a one-story used car lot called LA Motors. The "LA" stood for Larimer Avenue, a reference to Genovese's old Italian neighborhood in the city.[71] The lot was upgraded at great expense to the Pittsburgh family, and it was obvious this would be Genovese's permanent space. Genovese stayed at LA Motors daily

LA Motors. *U.S. government photograph.*

for a full eight-hour workday from 9:00 a.m. to 5:00 p.m. in his office that faced the car lot from Monday to Saturday.

He met with people in his office or at the restaurant across the street. He started to meet with Raucci and Porter again at his new place, on a daily basis, just as he had at the Holiday House. According to the FBI, Genovese was very hard to surveil at this location, due to a large number of his associates being in the area at all times. Nonetheless, the Pittsburgh office of the FBI installed a pole camera and was eventually able to bug the location's interior. Unfortunately for the FBI, Genovese had a habit of asking his associates to take a walk when the conversation started to get interesting. The FBI attempted to record the conversations outside, but these were drowned out by traffic noise, and only partial walk and talks were recorded from a tree that Genovese often stopped at while speaking.[72] Genovese was recorded speaking to mob members inside the car lot's office, but the conversations were not enough to indict him. According to the Pennsylvania Crime Commission, Genovese moved his headquarters after 1990—one more time before his death—to tiny Verona Auto Sales on the same street as the old LA Motors.[73] Genovese and his men also had a hunting camp owned by Jo Jo Pecora in Tionesta, Pennsylvania, called Charlie's Roost, where the guys would stay and hunt deer for a few weeks each year. This hunting camp also hosted some meetings with mobsters from out of town.

Genovese, Porter and Raucci would lead the Pittsburgh crime family into the promise-filled 1980s. However, despite their successes and profits over the next few years, there were already ominous signs of where the family's recent commitment to drugs and street taxes, led by Porter, would eventually take them. Pennsylvania state and federal authorities were already on the hunt for the drug dealers, suppliers and bookmakers who were feeding Genovese's alleged empire of vice in the tristate area.

BLOODY ALTOONA

I'm the Boss. I'm Jack Verilla. Cut his fingers off.

—alleged statement of John Verilla to Vincent Caracciolo[74]

THE MURDER OF JOHN CLARK

John Clark was a fifty-seven-year-old Altoona, Pennsylvania drug dealer, Salvation Army employee and Pittsburgh mob associate. Clark was angry that fifty-eight-year-old John "Jack" Verilla, a made member of Pittsburgh's Cosa Nostra and leader of a small crew of associates in Altoona, had cut him out of the drug business in 1978. Clark tried to compete with Verilla in distributing Quaaludes, Dilaudid and Percodan in Altoona and Pittsburgh, despite being told not to do so.[75] Clark threatened to tell the police about the crew's crimes if he was not let back in to earn. Clark also threatened the corrupt doctor Verilla was using to obtain the drugs. The doctor told Verilla's associate about the threat. Clark's tough talk was taken seriously, since he had participated in some of the group's worst offenses over the last few years and knew far too much. In January 1979, Verilla feared that if Clark confessed to the police, the media would find out and drag the names of the Pittsburgh hierarchy out into the open as well. Verilla had no doubt that such headlines would get him and his men killed by the secrecy-obsessed LaRocca, Mannarino and Genovese.[76] Fear was what motivated Verilla in

John Verilla. *Courtesy of the Pennsylvania State Archives.*

most of his major decisions, and Verilla was deeply afraid of the powerful and dangerous men at the top. Verilla's fear and lack of calm under pressure is what would drive him to make many poor calls.

Verilla met up with his top two associates, sixty-one-year-old John Caramadre and forty-eight-year-old Vincent Caracciolo, at their regular hangout and criminal headquarters of Jay's Bar in Altoona. The tiny bar was where many of their criminal schemes were hatched. Jay's was an unassuming place of great importance in the Altoona underworld of the late 1970s and early 1980s. Verilla and his men had congratulated and supported their criminal associates here after successes that brought them profit and power. This time, they were meeting to discuss what to do with their former partner. Caramadre, Verilla's most trusted adviser, did not want to kill Clark at first. Verilla argued for the death penalty based on his aforementioned fear of the don in Pittsburgh and added in that Caramadre was not well liked by the Pittsburgh hierarchy: "You know we're dead. You know they don't like you over there." Caramadre gave in to Verilla's reasoning and stated, "We'll kill him."[77]

Later the same day, Verilla, Caramadre and Caracciolo went to Caramadre's apartment to plan how they would kill Clark. Caramadre told Caracciolo to shoot Clark in a secluded area, and Verilla added that the murder should occur in Cambria County so his Blair County crew wouldn't be implicated. Caramadre dug around in a bag of guns he had stashed in his place and gave Caracciolo an untraceable handgun. Caracciolo recruited four people to help with the "roofing job," Caracciolo's code phrase for murder, and an associate lured Clark with the promise of a "pay day" in Johnstown for an unspecified criminal job.[78] Clark drove his own car, while Caracciolo and his four associates drove in another vehicle toward the meetup on a deserted road just over the Cambria County line at Mineral Point.[79] Caracciolo didn't plan to use Caramadre's gun. Once they arrived on the isolated roadside stop, Caracciolo's associates grabbed Clark, tied his hands with wire and placed a paper bag over his head. Caracciolo came up behind his helpless victim and brutally sank an axe into his skull. Caracciolo yanked the axe out of Clark's head and struck him several more times. The deed was done, and Clark and his vehicle were set on fire after being doused

Left: John Caramadre. *Right*: Vincent Caracciolo. *Courtesy of the Pennsylvania State Archives.*

with gasoline. Clark's burned and mutilated body was found by police in the burning car at Mineral Point, Cambria County, on January 23, 1979, the same day he was murdered.

Caracciolo returned to Jay's Bar, and Verilla greeted him with a hug and kiss on the cheek. Verilla told Caracciolo that he had done a "good job" and noted, "This is how we take care of our problems."[80] Verilla started to call Caracciolo "Little Al," in reference to the infamous Al Capone.

VERILLA'S RISE

Clark's murder was the consequence of a planned yearslong attempt by Verilla to reestablish control over the rackets in Altoona. According to informant testimony, Verilla was made into the Pittsburgh crime family sometime in the early 1950s and was given Altoona to run under Johnstown capo Little Joe Regino. Verilla and Caramadre had known each other since at least the 1950s, when they owned the Sixth Avenue Grille together in Altoona as of 1957.[81]

According to FBI files, Verilla appears to have had a short stint as an informant for the bureau. Multiple mob members talked to the FBI in the 1960s, as the bureau started to pay attention to organized crime. A few seemed to be naive about what the FBI was interested in, although Verilla's intentions for talking are not apparent from the documents. In 1968, the leader of the Cosa Nostra in Altoona, their name redacted in the report but documented as Verilla in other sources at the time, told the FBI that he had talked to Mike Genovese on the phone about drugs coming into Altoona from Johnstown after two women overdosed. Verilla appeared to be against the drugs, and Genovese stated he would look into stopping the trade. Verilla also described to the FBI that LaRocca and Genovese were pressuring him for more money coming out of the Altoona rackets since he was not making as much on numbers, horse racing and sports bets as usual. Verilla was very worried about this and was nervous that the hierarchy would back some unnamed rivals to take over the town. He stated outright that if this happened, he would have to retaliate and start a gang war to keep his turf.[82]

Verilla came down with some unspecified health problems from 1970 to 1973. Later in life, he would suffer from a blood sugar disorder and heart issues.[83] This interlude allowed a lot of independent operators to start up in Altoona, and Verilla lost some power and respect due to illness. In 1976, Verilla was healthy again and ready to resume his duties as the overlord of Altoona's underworld. Verilla obtained permission from the Pittsburgh hierarchy, represented by underboss Kelly Mannarino, to take things over again. He enlisted the help of Caramadre and Caracciolo. Caramadre was a longtime mafia associate, Verilla business partner, restaurateur and illegal gambling fixture, while Caracciolo was a somewhat successful owner of a home remodeling business and a more recent fixture in the Altoona underworld.

In 1976, the three men gathered in Caramadre's apartment to discuss a strategy to take over Altoona's rackets at a meeting that Caracciolo claimed lasted seven hours. They also outlined their roles in the new mob crew. Verilla acted as the local boss, Caramadre was the main advisor or counselor and Caracciolo was the lead enforcer. The strategy worked, and after a fairly brief period, they had an illegal gambling operation going and a new drug enterprise. The money was rolling in, and unfortunately for them, so was the drama.[84]

In many ways, the setting for this drama was an out-of-the-ordinary place for a fairly active mob crew to make a home. Altoona is a small city nestled in the mountains of western Pennsylvania at the edge of the Pittsburgh mafia's turf in the 1980s, 1990s and into the 2000s. Altoona is just under one hundred miles away from the Steel City in rural Blair County. The city was defined by the railroad industry, which declined as the industrial heartland of America declined in the 1980s and 1990s. However, Altoona still had other businesses that generated good income for the locals, like the headquarters of the Boyer candy company, the headquarters of the Sheetz gas station franchise, the Altoona branch of Pennsylvania State University and a thriving healthcare presence through the University of Pittsburgh Medical Center system. This was much more than other troubled cities in the area, like Youngstown and Johnstown, had to fall back on. At its height in 1930, Altoona had a population of about eighty thousand. From the late 1970s to the present day, Altoona's population has hovered from above fifty thousand to about forty-five thousand, with one hundred thousand people living close by in the Altoona suburbs. Altoona even has a small Little Italy neighborhood that represents the approximately 12 percent of Altoona's residents who identify as ethnic Italians.

A Prescription for Disaster

Verilla did not limit himself to dealing with only ethnic Italians. He needed criminal talent fast. He found some Italians who fit the bill but also recruited from other ethnicities, too. The drug enterprise the Verilla crew set up exemplified this and involved osteopath Dr. John Maras, who wrote the group thousands of bogus prescriptions for Dilaudid, Quaaludes and Percodan. Maras was aided by Howard "Tony" Hugar, a former Altoona police officer and Salvation Army Men's Social Service Center drug counselor who used his position to feed his clients' drug addictions by directing them to Maras. Clark also supplied the Maras operation with drugs for a while.[85] The Maras operation was so successful that the crew had an honorary dinner for Maras at one of their favorite restaurants, the Red Bull Inn. Verilla had gone from lecturing Genovese on the Cosa Nostra rule against drug dealing in 1968 to dealing them himself in 1978.

The drug business was a risk for the mobsters, since the community and law enforcement did not see drugs as a harmless vice like gambling. The penalties were also stiff and could force one of Verilla's associates into becoming an informant. This is what happened in 1978, after just two years of Verilla's rule in Altoona. Dennis Hileman was a thirty-three-year-old former medical assistant turned addict and one of the crew's drug customers. Hileman had been picked up by the Altoona police on a drug charge and offered to become an informant in return for leniency. The problem was that he was not very good at working undercover and simply started to hang around Jay's bar, trying to get close to Verilla and was very obvious while doing it. Verilla knew he was an informant since his corrupted contacts in the Altoona police had given him a heads up. Verilla tried to ignore Hileman, but one day in 1978, Verilla was complaining to Caracciolo about Hileman when he threw his glasses down on the bar and said, "Kill him. Kill him."[86]

Caracciolo did as asked. He had his own reason for disliking Hileman. Caracciolo suspected that Hileman had burglarized his apartment. Caracciolo stabbed Hileman in the back and then repeatedly beat him on the head with a masonry hammer, puncturing his skull multiple times. Caracciolo then paid two associates, Preston Ryan and Scott Brunner, both in their twenties, fifty bucks each to help get rid of the body. Caracciolo stated that the crew had a few thousand dollars in cash stashed away to use for any odd jobs like this that were necessary for the mob.[87] Ryan was a weightlifter and the perfect example of a non-Italian associate who felt an affinity for the Italian mafia and was allowed to immerse himself in it through the Pittsburgh family. Ryan helped maim and kill people for the family but also talked about the mafia code of not playing around with each other's women, being loyal and not lying to each other. The three men bound Hileman's body up with chains, wrapped it in a tarp and weighed it down with concrete blocks. Hileman's body was then dropped into the Tipton Reservoir. Caracciolo told Verilla that Hileman was dead at Jay's Bar. Verilla was overjoyed and stated, "This should make us look strong." Verilla was also satisfied that the police would think twice before trying to penetrate his crew with an informant.[88]

Dealing with Competition

The gambling business was vital to the Pittsburgh mob and was no less so for Verilla's Altoona operation. An associate, Joseph "the Weep" Ruggiero, oversaw Verilla's $300,000 a year numbers operation. Ruggiero and Verilla split the take right down the middle. A grand jury identified about a dozen small businesses that were fronts for the mob's illegal gambling in Altoona. One of the fronts was a pool hall with no pool tables—although there were some people hanging around who would take a bet for a customer. A pricey bet would necessitate a call out to New Kensington to lay it off with that faction's operation. New Kensington's illegal gambling presence was dominant in this era and before. New Kensington was described by the Pennsylvania Crime Commission as the "hub of a national layoff system" in its 1970 report.[89]

New Kensington was also the home of powerful Pittsburgh family underboss Gabriel "Kelly" Mannarino. Mannarino was also Verilla's boss and the guy Verilla consulted over the phone and in person when he needed advice. As was previously mentioned, Mannarino had given Verilla permission to reassert himself in Altoona. However, he also reined him in as needed. In the late 1970s, Verilla attempted to take over Paul Folcarelli's football betting operation in Altoona. According to the Pennsylvania Crime Commission, Folcarelli appealed to Mannarino for help, and Mannarino told Verilla to back off the lucrative venture. Caracciolo related that Verilla took him to see Mannarino twice in the late 1970s before Mannarino passed away. Verilla and Caracciolo traveled up to New Kensington's Catoris Candy Company, where Mannarino held court. Using the candy store as his headquarters was certainly a good idea and in line with how the secretive Mannarino did business. Who would suspect nefarious activities while they picked up a chocolate bar?

On the first visit, Mannarino and Verilla talked quietly out of earshot of Caracciolo for several hours while he waited next to a water cooler. At the end of the meeting, Verilla called him over and introduced him to Mannarino as "my right-hand man." Mannarino patted Caracciolo on the back and said "good boy" and told him to take care of Verilla.[90] According to the crime commission, Verilla paid 10 percent of his profits up to Mannarino until his

Catoris Candies in New Kensington. *Courtesy of the Pennsylvania State Archives.*

death and then to Sonny Ciancutti after that. After Mannarino died in 1980, soon to be made man Thomas "Sonny" Ciancutti took over his role as the mafia's lead in New Kensington.

Verilla's gambling operation in Altoona ran fairly smoothly for the first few years—except for a few incidents. Caracciolo and his thugs had to beat a few outsiders who tried to set up their own gambling operations in town, but there were no serious challenges until March 1978. At that time, Joseph "the Weep" Ruggiero reported that a Conrail employee named Joseph McDermott, who transited between Pittsburgh and Altoona, started a competing gambling operation at the Roundhouse Inn while he was in town. Verilla was livid and wanted to make an example of the interloper. Caramadre counseled caution, but Verilla overruled him. Verilla wanted to "teach everybody a lesson" and cut one of McDermott's fingers off since he had "greedy fingers."

Caracciolo and Clark abducted McDermott from an Altoona street and bundled him into a van after one of their associates identified him. Caracciolo then cut off McDermott's left pinky finger with a machete. Caracciolo brought the finger back to Verilla, and the mere sight of it made Verilla giddy with delight. Verilla wanted to call his superiors in Pittsburgh to tell them about the incident but thought better of it given how late at night it was. Verilla also toyed with preserving the finger as a grim trophy but told Caracciolo to get rid of it in the end. Caracciolo simply flicked it out his car window as he was driving down the street.[91]

In January 1981, Ernest Martz, a convenience store owner and bookie for Verilla, was found to be underreporting his profits to Verilla. Martz's car was burned and his house shot at one night. Martz appeared at Jay's Bar the next morning, hat in hand, and apologized to Verilla. Verilla and his crew were happy with this outcome, as it showed that their violent strategy was working.

Loansharking, or loans with extremely high interest rates that were collected through threats and violence if not paid on time, was also part of the crew's business strategy. Up-and-coming criminals who wanted cash to start up something illegal or gamblers and addicts who could not pay their debts were the main customers of these loans, as they were meant for people who had to avoid a regular bank.

Verilla's turf also had overlaps with the territories of two other made members who were much more low-key than the impulsive Verilla. Samuel Fashionatta was described by the Pennsylvania Crime Commission as a "close associate" of Verilla who had helped Verilla distribute football betting slips

Johnstown's resident capo until his death in 1985, Joseph Regino, in a surveillance photograph. *Courtesy of the Pennsylvania State Archives.*

and lived in Altoona. Fashionatta was also an illegal gambling facilitator in Johnstown and was involved with the locally famous Shangri-La Restaurant just outside of town on the lower slopes of Laurel Mountain. Fashionatta often oversaw the Johnstown rackets when Little Joe Regino was out of town in Florida.[92] Fashionatta died in 1985. Michael Traficante was the other made member who lived in Altoona, and he reportedly ran illegal gambling in Indiana County before he died in 1986.[93] After Regino died in 1985, Johnstown's importance to the family seems to have diminished, although the Pennsylvania Crime Commission lists Frederick Piera and Mike Gulino as mob associates who continued to operate there successfully. Gulino is described as a sports and numbers bookmaker whose operation could make up to $6 million in one football season. Piera reportedly ran his bookmaking business from the Clinton Street Recreation Center in Johnstown. It was estimated by the crime commission that Piera's operation could make up to $300,000 in two weeks. Johnstown was a quiet place for the mob, and the only documented murder associated with the crew that was committed there occurred in the 1960s, when bookie Pippy DiFalco was killed.[94]

Verilla also considered taking over the operations of mob associate Alfred Corbo. Corbo was allied with Verilla earlier in the 1970s but became a competitor. Corbo had a large and successful football, basketball and baseball betting operation in Altoona, and Verilla did not like that Corbo was independent of him. Verilla was even apparently ready to kill him. Verilla was told by the Pittsburgh hierarchy that he would leave Corbo alone, since Corbo was making more money for the family than Verilla at the time.[95] It was another humiliation that Verilla had to grin and bear.

THE BUSINESS OF BURNING

The crew also had a few odd misadventures and scores that are worth mentioning beyond the mainstays of drugs and gambling. In one instance, Verilla wanted to print off some football tickets and had two of Caracciolo's muscle men beat the printer with baseball bats until he acquiesced.[96] The crew also convinced Donald Black, a prominent State College insurance agent, to embezzle $250,000 from his clients and his firm. Verilla used some of the money to pay off debts incurred by the legitimate businesses owned by him and Caramadre.[97] The legitimate businesses owned by the crew included Jay's Bar and the Cara-Villa Ristorante. The Cara-Villa was owned, at least on paper, by Caramadre and Verilla's wife. John LaRocca may have also held an interest in it, per accusations from a Pennsylvania state prosecutor who implied in court that the aging don had bought the kitchen equipment for the place. Roma Enterprises Incorporated was also under Verilla and had an address that matched that of his home. The company had purchased property from Verilla and Caracciolo in 1980.[98]

Caracciolo's death blows from a hammer and axe weren't the only intimidation tactics used by the family. Arson was a means of enforcing the crew's will and a new way to make money. The crew torched a disco in 1978, when the owner reneged on a deal that he would share the place with the mob. In another instance, an Altoona customer who had taken a loan from Verilla's crew was behind on his payments and the 10 percent weekly interest he owed. The mob torched his garage; they did not want him to fall further behind on his payments, and if they torched his house, he would have to rent a new one. The garage's insurance money was collected by the man's mortgage company before Verilla saw a cent, so the mob got stiffed.

Sister Bernice Shaw was a member of a religious order that had a state contract to provide a summer lunch program for underprivileged kids. In 1979, mishandled funds led the state to cut off the money to the program named Noah's Ark. Sister Shaw did not accept blame and instead pointed a finger at organized crime during a press conference. The Verilla crew had not done anything, and they were angry that Shaw blamed the mafia for the issue. Verilla decided to take vengeance and torched the Noah's Ark building. Sister Shaw was not the only reason cited for the destruction. Caramadre's racism came out when he allegedly commented that the place was near his house and he thought it attracted too many Black people. As a result, he was glad to be rid of it. Caramadre even had his men burn down his own garage since it needed to be repaired and it was cheaper to simply raze it.

Caracciolo also stated that the crew would take arson jobs from businessmen and individuals who wanted to collect the insurance money for a 10 percent cut. The percentage had to be paid immediately, or the client risked a not so friendly visit from Caracciolo. One of Caracciolo's bumbling arson clients owned a failing AG Market in Altoona. Brian McCord also co-owned five Dairy Queens in the area. McCord did not like that Caracciolo wanted $25,000 to torch his store. McCord drove over to some townhomes he was selling with Caracciolo, Caracciolo's girlfriend and another individual. McCord wanted to sell Caracciolo the homes with a $50,000 discount rather than pay the $25,000 outright for the proposed fire. Caracciolo did not go for the deal. McCord was desperate and did the job himself. The store burned, but the insurance company ruled the fire suspicious and McCord did not get his payday. McCord's fire also almost killed a tenant in the building, caused injuries to a fireman who never went back to his job and put McCord's three market workers out of their jobs. McCord's prosecutor made it a point to state that while McCord was looking for a $200,000 payday, he was not exactly poor, as he drove a Mercedes Benz in working-class Altoona.[99] McCord was found guilty in 1986.

JUSTICE

On November 26, 1979, the badly decomposed body of Dennis Hileman was pulled from the Tipton Reservoir. The murder of the one-time police informant, medical assistant and drug addict, combined with the discovery of Clark's burning corpse in Mineral Point that same year, was enough to get law enforcement to ask what was going on in Blair County. Arsons were also popping up all over, and it was clear someone was aggressively moving in the underworld in this lightly populated and mostly rural area. By 1981, Blair County had formed a grand jury to look into the organized crime presence in Altoona and the surrounding territory. The Commonwealth of Pennsylvania was trying to come to grips with Verilla's crew and their "reign of terror."[100]

The state hired special prosecutor George Parry from Philadelphia, who had extensive experience in organized crime investigations, to direct the prosecution team. The grand jury itself was made up of Blair County citizens who had no clue that their little area was home to such a vicious group of criminals. They were shocked but determined. The grand jurors took copious notes from witnesses and victims and asked tough questions that surprised even the prosecutor. Their law enforcement partners consisted of a seven-man Pennsylvania state trooper team led by troopers Ed Pottmeyer and John Winklebauer. They recruited informants and tapped mobsters' phones in one of the largest wiretapping operations in Pennsylvania state history. They even operated for a month from an abandoned store in Altoona and did twelve-hour shifts for twenty-four-hour coverage on the gangsters' phones.

The first domino fell before the Blair County grand jury ever convened. Joseph Martino, an associate who helped Caracciolo murder Clark, agreed to cooperate against the group in March 1980, after he was arrested for armed robbery.[101] Marvin Wansley, another accomplice in the Clark murder, came next. Both wore wires to record conversations with the Verilla mobsters. The informants' recorders caught conversations with Verilla about his desire to go to jail rather than expose the rest of the mob and discussions with Caracciolo about a murder, an arson and a robbery. The tapes were damning evidence. Caracciolo was even captured on tape threatening Wansley, because he was apparently worried Wansley would cooperate with authorities. Caracciolo stated, "Whoever turns is dead," and, "You know if you panic, I can't let you get to court."

Verilla, Caramadre and Caracciolo clearly knew the probe was underway by the spring of 1982 and were desperate to avoid going to prison. As a result of the witness intimidation, the local judge held Verilla and Caracciolo on charges of solicitation to commit perjury, solicitation to commit false swearing and obstruction of justice. Caracciolo was also charged with intimidation of a witness. Verilla was let out of prison on a $500,000 bond, while Caracciolo was released on a $400,000 bond.[102] It is amazing they weren't put in jail until trial, given their history.

In July 1983, the proverbial axe finally fell on Verilla, Caramadre and Caracciolo. They were arrested and charged by the Commonwealth of Pennsylvania with murder, arson, kidnapping, loansharking, illegal gambling, drug trafficking, burglary and violation of Pennsylvania's corrupt organizations act.[103] The Verilla case was the first use of Pennsylvania's version of the federal RICO statute. Cooperating in the case were Martino and Wansley, as well as two other associates. Preston Ryan, who was a close friend of Caracciolo, also turned state's evidence. Caracciolo knew he had no chance of defending himself from the charges once Ryan turned. At this time, Verilla allegedly made the boneheaded move of threatening Caracciolo's girlfriend's life. She informed her boyfriend of the threat, and Caracciolo decided to reach out to Pottmeyer to testify against his accomplices. Caracciolo was placed in protective custody but was offered no deal for his testimony. Caracciolo would not get leniency at his sentencing for his information but would obtain vengeance and a purportedly cleaner conscience for his efforts. It was a bad cooperation deal, and one wonders if Caracciolo could have used a better lawyer, since he was about to make the state's case for them for nothing.

The trial started on September 10, 1984, in Ebensburg, which is also where Verilla was staying as a guest of the commonwealth at Cambria County Prison.[104] Caracciolo's testimony was damning, and to make matters worse, he looked cool, calm and confident with his blue pin-striped suit as he described, in a matter-of-fact way, his crime spree for the mob over the last seven or eight years. Verilla's only defense was whispering "lies" within hearing distance of the jury while the witnesses testified. The old man was described as having a perpetual frown, wrinkled pants, a soiled handkerchief hanging from his back pocket and a buttoned-down short sleeve shirt that was a little too tight around his belly. Verilla and his lawyer mentioned that he was a World War II veteran who served as a merchant marine near Guadalcanal, and they said he was an active worker in a hot lunch program for the poor. The mention of his service in the hot lunch program omitted that he had allowed Caramadre and Caracciolo to burn Noah's Ark down after Sister Shaw insulted the mob.

Verilla's lawyer also called two witnesses who claimed they met Caracciolo in prison and that he had told them that he was the real boss of the Altoona crew. The defense was blown up when the prosecutor called the witnesses out with documentation that proved they never served a day in prison with Caracciolo. The two men were arrested by police for perjury as they walked out of the courtroom.[105]

In October 1984, the jury found Verilla guilty of murder and the other lesser crimes. He was put up for the death penalty, but the jury was deadlocked on his punishment, so he was given life imprisonment instead. Verilla made a quick sign of the cross once he heard the state would not kill him. He then turned around to say goodbye to his weeping wife and family as the sheriff's deputies took him to prison. Caracciolo, despite his testimony,

The Altoona Mirror

Verilla (*left*) and Caramadre (*right*) in handcuffs. *Courtesy of the* Altoona Mirror.

would also be condemned to die behind bars, and Caramadre also got life imprisonment. The Blair County grand jury, Pennsylvania State Police and the special prosecutor George Parry had done an outstanding job. A state government managing such a complex organized crime prosecution so deftly was a rare thing, and it was done without significant federal assistance. Everyone involved could feel great about removing such a malevolent group of criminals from the streets of Altoona. The grand jury's work had led to sixty-five successful cases.[106] Verilla died in prison in 1988.

There was still one item left undone in the Verilla saga. The case had turned up public corruption allegations, according to the tapes and witnesses. Verilla had allegedly attempted to bribe the mayor of Altoona with an envelope full of cash, even though the mayor handed it back to him immediately. Caracciolo also stated the mob had a police captain on their payroll, and there were allegations that a city hall employee had stolen state documents for the crew. The corruption allegations do not appear to have gone anywhere in the years that Verilla and his team of criminals were being prosecuted. The special prosecutor George Parry also alleged that his crack team of state troopers were taken off the case and given traffic duty after Verilla was convicted, despite more work that needed to be done. The state contended this was false and that the troopers could still work their cases but that they also needed to do other more menial jobs. The corruption angle of the Verilla case was never adequately fleshed out.[107]

A New Leader

Alfred Corbo. *Courtesy of the Pennsylvania State Archives.*

The Pittsburgh mob hierarchy could probably be forgiven for feeling relieved when the trial ended and the less than stellar performance of Verilla could be put behind them. There was still money to be made in Altoona after all. The earlier decision to stop Verilla from taking control of or murdering talented and profitable mob associate Alfred Corbo now paid off in full. Corbo reportedly took over Verilla's rackets and kept his already diverse criminal portfolio. It seems Corbo was not affected by the Verilla prosecution in the least. Verilla's departure was likely the best thing for Altoona and Corbo.

According to the Pennsylvania Crime Commission, the media and Corbo's obituary, Corbo, a Korean War veteran, was convicted of nineteen counts of illegal gambling, bookmaking and conspiracy in January 1988. Law enforcement used an extensive wiretapping operation to uncover Corbo's gambling network. The conviction did not result in a long-term setback for Corbo's illegal business, which still relied on the profits from sports betting. The 1992 Pennsylvania Crime Commission report notes that Corbo was the alleged head of the Pittsburgh family's interests in Altoona in the 1990s. The commission claimed the Cosa Nostra had a complete lock on illegal gambling in Altoona and had a hand in loansharking, fencing and drug trafficking. Corbo paid a percentage of his profits to the Pittsburgh hierarchy for as long as he remained in the business.[108]

Corbo's alleged headquarters was Brunswick Billiards in Altoona. Competition was stamped out by Corbo's reported violent and retaliatory reputation in Altoona. He did not tolerate delinquent payments on loanshark loans, which were given out with 20 percent interest and backed by mob muscle. It seemed he was just as powerful as Verilla but did not have the overly aggressive and flashy moves that attracted law enforcement's scrutiny in the early 1980s. Corbo's alleged drug trafficking enterprises reportedly involved him using his private plane and his pilot's license to personally fly cocaine from West Virginia to Altoona for a cut of the profits. He also reportedly gave a loanshark loan to a drug dealer to enhance his cocaine distribution network. The same source said Corbo had a piece of the drug business undertaken by "the Seekers," a motorcycle gang chapter in Altoona. Public corruption also allegedly continued under Corbo, as was shown when he reportedly loaned money to a former Altoona police officer who could not pay him back. Corbo simply made the officer a mob mole who provided confidential information and performed favors for the organization. Corbo was also allegedly involved in a fencing operation based out of a local pawn shop.[109] In short, Corbo reportedly had his hand in every pie and only died in 2012 at the age of eighty-two.[110]

"LITTLE JOEY" NAPLES AND THE MAFIA WAR

Very professional and very dangerous.[111]

—*excerpt from an FBI Cleveland document describing one of Naples's hitmen*

THE RISE OF NAPLES

Joseph Naples Jr. was born in Youngstown, Ohio, on October 9, 1932. His family had allegedly been involved in illegal gambling since the 1930s, and he had been involved since the early 1950s. Little Joey was the youngest brother of four who were all involved in the rackets in Youngstown to varying degrees.[112] Sandy was the oldest brother and the boss of the Naples's gambling enterprise while Billy, the middle brother, was his second in command.

In the 1950s and 1960s, Youngstown was a confusing and brutal place for those involved in the "bug," the local numbers game. At the time, the Cleveland, Buffalo, Pittsburgh and even Detroit families participated in the Youngstown rackets. There was also an independent Calabrian faction in the city.[113]

The Naples brothers got into a conflict with another faction due to their insistence on not paying tribute and their aggressive moves into territory that was already claimed by others. The brothers also had vending machines that

A younger Joseph Naples
(*far left*). *Courtesy of an
anonymous researcher.*

they placed in businesses through negotiation and sometimes force. Little Joey's headquarters until the early 1990s was a place called Youngstown United Music Company. He used it to distribute vending machines and collect gambling profits.

In March 1960, Sandy's enemies caught up with him while he walked up to his girlfriend's house. He and his girlfriend were shot to death with a shotgun. Sandy fired six rounds from a handgun at his assailant before succumbing to his wounds.[114] Billy became the head of the faction. One night in July 1962, Billy was in a car parked in a Youngstown garage when a terrific explosion occurred that blew him partially out the back window and caused the roof of the garage to collapse onto his car. He was dead. Little Joey was in charge of the family business.[115]

In the same year as Billy's death, Little Joey went on trial after a raid on his house uncovered firearms, numbers slips and stolen property. The prosecutors, defense attorneys and judge were in a conference in the judge's chambers while the evidence remained in the courtroom. When the parties returned to the courtroom, they found all the evidence had been stolen. It was a stunning development that resulted in a delay in the trial. Despite this brazen act of sabotage, Naples was a convicted felon by the end of the 1960s. He even appealed one of his convictions to the U.S. Supreme Court but lost.[116]

Naples also expanded his vending machine business in the 1960s. The manner in which he did this varied, but the FBI files reveal how he forced unwilling businesses to place his machines in their buildings. In one example from the mid-1960s, Naples found a business and removed his competitor's machines without permission. He then put his machines in their place. The machines included a jukebox, a cigarette machine and a coin-operated pool table. The owners complained about the machines, as they did not want their business associated with Naples. The business first received a visit from a Youngstown councilman, who told them to keep the machines. The police then showed up to ask about the machines, with the implication being that they should keep them. After the possible police harassment, two "hoodlums" showed up and told them they should keep the machines. The business owners eventually went to the mayor's office, and Naples relented and removed the machines. He did not resort to violence to keep the machines there in this instance.[117]

Naples, despite his legal troubles, still had to worry about his safety in the 1960s. He had an associate build a novel device that is the very definition of necessity being the mother of invention. Youngstown was infamous at the time and was called "Crimetown" and "Bombtown" USA due to the inordinate number of racketeers who were killed by car bombs in the area. The bombing war came to national attention when Charlie Cavallaro, a racketeer, and his young son were blown up in a car bombing. The FBI got involved in Youngstown after the public outrage at the brutal death of a child.[118] One of Naples's friends came up with an ingenious way to beat the danger of car bombs. Naples explained the device to an FBI agent, saying it was a radio transmitter that could start a car from a block away, thus allowing him to avoid his brother Billy's fate. Naples was actually incredibly open and friendly with FBI agents in the 1960s, until they started to take law enforcement actions against him.[119]

Joseph Naples Jr.

Joseph Naples. *As printed in the* Pittsburgh Post-Gazette.

According to FBI informants, crossing Joey Naples was not wise. In February 1975, twenty-seven-year-old Karl Netolicky and another man were suspected by Naples of raping two go-go girls. Naples allegedly ordered an associate to kill the two men.[120] Netolicky was found in a ditch in Atwater Township with three bullet wounds to the head, and the other man was found gravely beaten with two gunshot wounds to the back and one to the head. Both men were almost naked except for their shirts.[121] Naples was arrested for the hit but released due to a lack of evidence against him.[122] Naples also allegedly ordered the burning of a Youngstown city councilman's car in 1979 as a message to him, since he was speaking out and urging police action against the rackets in his ward of the city.[123] In another example, a Naples hit man, Sam Fossesca, warned a Cleveland faction leader of Naples's intention to kill him, and he paid for that act by getting shot twice in the buttocks, once in each cheek. He was lucky he wasn't dead.[124]

Aligning with Prato and Pittsburgh

In 1964, Naples mentioned to an FBI agent who had stopped by to chat with him that Vincenzo "Two Gun Jimmy" Prato had attended his father's funeral. The aging Prato was next mentioned by the FBI in 1975 in the company of Naples and a potential Youngstown mayoral candidate. Prato was the nephew of the Calabrian faction leader Dominick Mallamo and a made member of the Pittsburgh family who represented their interests in the Youngstown area. Prato's headquarters was a restaurant and bar named the Calla-Mar Manor. By the late 1970s, Naples and Prato were joined at the hip, working to expand the interests of the Pittsburgh family in the

The remains of Prato's Calla-Mar Manor in 2022. *Courtesy of an anonymous researcher.*

greater Youngstown area. An uneasy peace had reigned in Youngstown in the 1970s, with Ronald Carabbia, his brothers and a few others in charge of the Youngstown-area rackets for the Cleveland family. Cleveland and Pittsburgh were the only two factions left in Youngstown by the 1970s.

THE CLEVELAND FAMILY STUMBLES

At the same time, the don of the Cleveland mob James "Jack White" Licavoli was engaged in a war with insurgent Irish gang leader Danny Greene. Greene and Licavoli were busy killing each other's men in a war that rocked Cleveland in the mid- to late 1970s. The war diverted Cleveland's attention, caused the deaths of valuable men and gave law enforcement a reason to crack down on the mob. In October 1977, Ronald Carabbia led a hit team that set off a remote-control car bomb that blew Greene up after a dentist appointment.[125] The troublesome Irish gangster was dead, but shortly thereafter, many Cleveland mob members and associates were arrested for Greene's murder or on racketeering charges. Licavoli was now beset with legal problems that allowed Cleveland underboss Angelo Lonardo to step up and take care of relations with the Pittsburgh family. Carabbia's incarceration after the Greene hit left his brothers and the Cleveland faction in Youngstown vulnerable. Naples and Prato smelled blood and started to move to take over what remained of Cleveland's piece of the action. According to FBI and local law enforcement informants, they had sanction from underboss Kelly Mannarino to make a move on Cleveland's interests in the area.

TRAFICANT'S ROLE

The new mob war would be fought on the streets of Youngstown between the mortally weakened Cleveland mafia faction and the resurgent Pittsburgh mafia faction. At the same time the war was raging, Youngstown's economy was in a freefall due to the closing of major steel concerns in the city and surrounding areas. It was a dangerous time. The casualty numbers in the war would be on par with those of the infamous Colombo family war of the early 1990s in New York. The prize was the millions of dollars in profit to be made in the Mahoning Valley rackets and control of the multitude of corrupt politicians.

There was no politician more brazenly and unapologetically corrupt than the new sheriff of Mahoning County, James Traficant. Traficant waded right into the middle of the conflict between the factions. Traficant won the primary and general elections for sheriff in an upset in 1980. Before he took office, he met with Charles and Orlando Carabbia, the brothers of the former Cleveland leader Ronald, to talk about the $163,000 in illegal campaign contributions he had taken from both the Cleveland and Pittsburgh mafia factions in Youngstown.

Unknown to Traficant, one of the mobsters was recording the conversation, and the FBI eventually got their hands on the tapes. Traficant was very specific during his conversation with the Carabbias that he would go after the Pittsburgh operations with his police powers to help them. He and the organized crime brothers then went on to talk about all the politicians and which faction they stood with.[126] The FBI called Traficant in to talk to him about the tapes, and when they played them for him, his usually boisterous manner deflated, and he agreed to sign a confession admitting guilt to mafia-related corruption of his office. However, Traficant decided to go back on his confession and fight the charges in court as his own lawyer once he found out he would not get to serve out his term as sheriff.[127]

The trial was a sideshow spectacle, with Traficant casting doubt on the written confession as a fake, calling the FBI agents liars and convincing the jury to not trust the frankly amazing evidence on the tapes. He also ludicrously stated that he was performing a one-man sting operation on both mob families and had to take the money to complete the ruse. The area and some of its citizens had been suspicious of the government for some time due to their economic misfortunes and other factors. Sheriff Traficant seemed to some to be a man of the people, a local boy done good, and they thought he was getting screwed by the feds. Traficant preyed on their suspicions of the federal government for his own benefit. Traficant knew how to pull out the populist rhetoric and pull on the heartstrings as well. A case that should have been open and shut was not, and the jury acquitted Traficant of the federal charges in June 1983. Traficant would go back to his corrupt ways as the area's longtime congressman. The jury had ignored what was a mountain of incredible evidence and based their decision not on the law but on how they felt personally about the man before them and his politics.[128] Traficant wasn't alone in his corruption; many valley officials were implicated as working with the mob, including unsubstantiated allegations about a former FBI agent turned local law enforcement leader who was potentially compromised by Naples.

The riddle of Youngstown

Another last stand for Traficant and his city

By Bill Heltzel
Post-Gazette Staff Writer

YOUNGSTOWN, Ohio — It would be an extraordinary moment in most any city except Youngstown.

Indicted U.S. Rep. James Traficant Jr. will be the host of a radio talk show this week on which he has promised to disclose evidence of FBI corruption in northeastern Ohio.

It is not the attack on federal agents that will be extraordinary. Traficant, a maverick Democrat, has done that before, beginning 20 years ago when he was charged with bribery and tax evasion, and more recently while a federal strike force investigated him on new racketeering accusations.

The radio stint will be significant because Traficant is the embodiment of one of the country's most unusual political cultures and because Youngstown is at a crossroads.

He has dominated Youngstown politics for 20 years, first as sheriff and the last 16 years as congressman. He has embraced the region's gritty working class ethos. He has tried tirelessly to reverse 25 years of economic stagnation, though critics say he is actually the chief obstacle to growth. And his name is frequently mentioned when the region is cited as one of the most corrupt in America.

There are signs of change.

SEE **YOUNGSTOWN,** PAGE A-16

US MARSHAL
YOUNGSTOWN OH
31213 --060
S II 01

Rep. James Traficant Jr. in his FBI portrait — Retirees around Youngstown say he is the rare politician who fights for the working man.

James Traficant's mug shot. *U.S. Marshals' photograph, as printed in the* Pittsburgh Post-Gazette.

A new generation of prosecutors would go after the cagey congressman in 2002. He was accused of forcing his aides to work on his farm, carry out menial chores and solicit bribes from mob-connected businessmen for government favors. Once again, Traficant railed against the allegations on television and defended himself in court. This time, he lost and was sent to prison for seven years and expelled from Congress. He ran for his old seat as an independent but lost to a former aide. The magic was gone, and the Mahoning Valley was wiser than it had been in 1983. He was released in 2009 and died in 2014 after a tractor accident. The colorful, corrupt, talented and charismatic congressman was able to beat the system for almost twenty years after his acquittal in the mafia bribery case, but justice eventually caught up with him.[129]

Mahoning Massacre

By the late 1970s, underworld politics and diplomacy had failed to avert violent conflict, even after Licavoli and Lonardo tried to quiet the simmering tensions.[130] According to the *Youngstown Vindicator*, in the fall of 1977, Licavoli met with Mannarino in New Kensington and told him that the Carabbias were with him and that Prato and Naples should not touch them. According to FBI affidavits, Naples reportedly ordered two of his associates, Charles

"Spider" Grisham and James "Peeps" Cononico, to take over the Warren, Ohio gambling rackets of Cleveland faction member Joseph Perfette. Naples thought Perfette would fold and that Cleveland don Licavoli had too much on his plate already to defend against Naples's moves. Licavoli wasn't ready to fold, and he ordered the death of Grisham and Cononico. Joseph DeRose Jr., a Cleveland-aligned mobster from the local area, was given the contract. Grisham and Cononico started to muscle in on Perfette. Grisham was shot to death in December 1978 outside of his home in the early morning hours by a gunman who had been hiding behind a bush next to his apartment. In January 1979, Cononico was walking from his truck to a drug treatment facility halfway house in Youngstown when he was shot in the chest and died. The war had started.[131]

At first, the Naples faction seemed to be getting the worst of it; although, there is information that the next hit was ordered by Naples and was allegedly internal house cleaning. Robert Furey was an employee of Naples's mob front Youngstown United Music and a convicted kidnapper, rapist and burglar. Furey was in his car outside his home repairing a tire in April 1979, when he was shot twice in the head and died.[132] An informant stated that the Furey contract was put out by Naples, since Furey was skimming money from Naples's operation. The hit was allegedly conducted by Pittsburgh faction hit man Sam Scaffidi. Scaffidi had reportedly punctured Furey's tire as part of the setup for the murder.

In July 1979, Naples's ally John Tobin was walking to his suburban Austintown apartment when he was shot to death after apparently engaging in a firefight with his killers, given that his revolver was determined to have been fired several times. Police described him as one of the area's biggest bookmakers and the owner of Somebody's Restaurant.[133] According to the *Youngstown Vindicator*, in January 1980, law enforcement discovered the body of Tobin's debt collector, John Magda, in a dump in Struthers, Ohio.[134] Magda's hands and feet were bound with flex cuffs, and his head and upper torso were wrapped so tightly with carpet tape that his nose had been broken. Magda died of asphyxiation.

The leadership of the two families were still speaking during the very localized war. In February 1980, Pittsburgh members Mannarino, Prato, Pasquale Ferruccio and Thomas Ciancutti met with Cleveland leaders Licavoli and Lonardo at the Brown Derby Inn off Exit 12 of the Ohio Turnpike. However, whatever was discussed, the killing did not stop.

As 1980 began, it was the turn of the Cleveland faction, led by the remaining Carabbia brothers, to feel the pain. On Valentine's Day 1980, thirty-six-year-old Carabbia loyalist Robert DeCerbo was sitting and watching TV in his living room in Beaver Township when shotgun blasts tore through his window and killed him.[135] There was also a police theory that DeCerbo had changed sides and was killed by the Cleveland faction for his disloyalty. DeCerbo had also survived a car bombing in 1978.

According to FBI documents, a little before midnight on October 2, 1980, Dominic "Junior" Senzarino pulled into his garage through the automatic garage door. Senzarino was the cousin of Ronald Carabbia, the imprisoned leader of Youngstown's Cleveland faction and a convicted burglar. The hit man was either already in Senzarino's garage or had slipped in as the automatic door shut. Senzarino exited his car and was killed by a shotgun blast to the head. Three expended shotgun shells were found at the scene. The closing door must have trapped the attacker, since he had to break the garage window to get out and cut himself on the glass, leaving a half-mile-long blood trail the police were able to follow to a point. Long after Senzarino's death, a Cleveland family associate stated Orlando Carabbia ordered the murder due to Senzarino paying a portion of his underworld income to the Pittsburgh family without Cleveland's permission.

The next target for Naples and Prato was a bigger fish named Joseph DeRose Jr. DeRose had connections to both the Cleveland and Pittsburgh factions, and Naples thought DeRose had been given the contract to kill Naples by Cleveland mafia powerhouse and drug ringleader Joseph Gallo. DeRose was also suspected of being involved in some of the other murders, even one of the murders of a Cleveland faction operative.

All that mattered was that Naples thought DeRose was gunning for him, so DeRose was marked for death. Naples took killing DeRose seriously, and according to government informants, Naples rented an apartment close to DeRose's residence so he and another hit man could surveil him more effectively. Naples also had alleged hit man Paul Holovatick tap DeRose's phone along with some of his associates to better track DeRose and the Carabbias. The taps were also recorded, and Holovatick even had a tape of the Cleveland faction discussing their plans to murder Naples. On the night of May 14, 1980, as DeRose and a date walked up to his Canfield, Ohio home, a car sped up, and gunmen shot at DeRose and his girl. DeRose was wounded three times, as was his girlfriend. They both lived through the attack.

Further information on the failed assassination would come to light a few years later when Naples's hit man Peter Cascarelli, who later stopped cooperating with authorities, stated that Naples ordered DeRose's death and told the hitmen that if anyone was with him, they should be killed, too,

Joe DeRose Jr. *Courtesy of an anonymous researcher.*

so there were no witnesses. Cascarelli started to cooperate since he thought the notoriously violent Naples was going to kill him for failing to kill DeRose and for dropping his silenced .22 handgun at the scene of the crime.[136]

In February 1981, Joseph DeRose Sr., the father of Joseph DeRose Jr., drove his son's car to his home in Boardman Township. As he exited the vehicle, he was killed by a shotgun blast. Police believed that the father was mistaken for the son due to the father's use of his son's car on that night.[137] In April 1981, the thirty-two-year-old DeRose left his mother's house and was never seen again. The car he drove that night, a 1976 Pontiac, was found burning in Peninsula, Ohio, with no one in it.[138] Shortly after the disappearance, an FBI bug caught Prato and another man talking about DeRose's disappearance and mentioning details that were only known by law enforcement at the time.[139] In 2002, Samuel Fossesca was indicted for the murder of DeRose after his associates provided testimony against him as a result of their arrests for a theft ring investigation. DeRose's body has never been found.[140]

The most important Cleveland faction member who remained alive in 1980 was Charles Carabbia. Carabbia had made the incriminating tapes of Traficant and was supposed to help run the rackets, pay the politicians, pay Licavoli and make money for his imprisoned brother Ronnie's family while he was away for the murder of Danny Greene. Instead, Charlie kept himself busy badmouthing Naples, Prato and the hierarchies of both the Cleveland and Pittsburgh families. A drunk Carabbia would shoot his mouth off at the local bars while the wrong people heard him. He was also allegedly not paying the full 25 percent of his gambling profits up to the Cleveland family, which enraged Licavoli. The split was supposed to be 25 percent for the Carabbias, 25 percent for Cleveland and 50 percent for the Pittsburgh faction. Naples and Prato heard about the outbursts against them and became concerned that Carabbia himself would make a move. They complained up their chain to Mannarino, who complained to the aging LaRocca.

According to Cleveland underboss and later acting boss Angelo Lonardo, the two families called a meeting between the highest levels to discuss

Carabbia. Other meetings had preceded this one, and Cleveland had always argued for their representative and insisted that he was needed to lead their interests in the area.

However, in 1980, Lonardo traveled with Canton, Ohio resident and made Pittsburgh member Pasquale Ferruccio to see Mannarino and LaRocca at Mannarino's house. LaRocca and Mannarino made it clear they wanted Carabbia eliminated, although all agreed to give Carabbia one more chance. However, if he crossed Pittsburgh again, LaRocca and Mannarino stated Carabbia would be killed without consulting with Cleveland a second time.[141] Carabbia did not last long. Pittsburgh had a trusted associate give a call to Carabbia to get him to a meeting at the Stardust Motel in Beaver Township, Ohio. After December 1980, when the meeting allegedly took place, neither Carabbia nor his body would ever be seen again. Pittsburgh apologized to Lonardo and stated it could not be helped and that Carabbia was going to kill Prato and Naples. They also apologized that Carabbia's car had been dumped in Cleveland.[142] DeRose and Carabbia's deaths left Naples and Prato in command of the whole area. Some loose ends needed to be tied up, but the Pittsburgh faction had clearly won the war. Orlando Carabbia, the last brother, was arrested on drug charges in 1983.[143]

HOME INVASION

In the meantime, the FBI was trying to stop the bloodshed, which was already winding down, and dent the Pittsburgh family's robust operations in the greater Youngstown area. They had installed a bug at Prato's headquarters in the Calla-Mar Manor and in Naples's hit man Sam Scaffidi's car. They also put a bug in the Standard Motors building on Andrews Avenue, where Scaffidi and his associates planned a new score. The car he used in the job was a station wagon that a former government witness had identified as the vehicle used to stalk DeRose Jr. while Naples's crew was hunting him. According to the FBI, Scaffidi was suspected in at least four gangland hits for the Naples faction. He was one of their most prolific enforcers and did not hesitate to use violence.

Paul Piater was not involved in the rackets; he was in his seventies and kept busy running Long's Greenhouse in Youngstown, Ohio. Rumor had it that he had stashed valuable coins and cash in a safe and around his house. Scaffidi and his associates had heard about the alleged items and decided

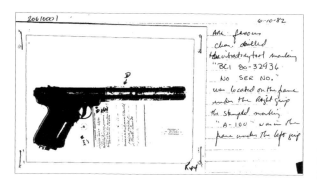

A photograph of Scaffidi's silenced .22 handgun. *FBI photograph.*

to execute a home invasion to steal what they likely thought would be a big score. Scaffidi and his associates had a female accomplice call the greenhouse and make a vegetable order that her "husband" would come by and pick up at night on June 4, 1982. Piater was ready when Scaffidi and his men pulled up for the vegetables.

As he was conversing with the driver of the station wagon, Piater was shot with a taser and grabbed from behind. However, Piater had a .38 revolver in his back pocket and managed to retrieve it and attempt to fire at the person who was on his back. Piater shot his own finger off. Piater was subdued by the men after the shooting, and his head, mouth, eyes and nose were wrapped in duct tape. They then took him into the basement and handcuffed him to a chair. Scaffidi had a .22 handgun with a silencer and an obliterated serial number during the robbery, so the group may have planned to kill Piater once they obtained their loot. Piater later explained that the coins in his house and safe were not actually worth much and that the valuable coin collection the subjects were looking for was no longer in the home.[144] The FBI leaped into action when they realized what was going on after listening to the plotting mobsters on their wires in Scaffidi's car and at Standard Motors. The assailants tried to escape but were caught and imprisoned. Scaffidi went away on a felon in possession of a firearm charge, and the FBI had removed one of Naples's hit teams by foiling the home invasion.

In the meantime, the bug in Prato's Calla-Mar Manor was working just fine until the FBI decided to add video to the audio setup. The installation of the video did not go well. In 1981, a leaky roof caused Prato to call a repairman, and the mobsters discovered the two microphones and a camera in the ceiling. Prato refused to give the equipment back when FBI agents arrived to pick it up and even ordered the police chief of Beaver Township to evict the agents from the premises. The equipment was finally recovered after the agents got a court order.[145]

In the mid-1980s, alleged Pittsburgh consigliere Charles Imburgia negotiated with what remained of the Cleveland Cosa Nostra on the street. There wasn't much left in Cleveland after so many were killed and imprisoned in the late 1970s and early 1980s. Imburgia's task was to split gambling profits with Cleveland in Ohio's Trumbull County right down the middle. This deal remained in effect until the principal gambling operators in the area were arrested in 1990.[146]

Naples and Prato had taken a lot of risks, but by 1983, they were the masters of eastern Ohio. The lion's share of the profits was going to them and their bosses in Pittsburgh. It had taken a mob war that claimed nine or ten lives, give or take the Furey hit, including killed and wounded innocents. The war also resulted in extra heat on Naples and Prato and the arrest of Scaffidi and his crew of enforcers. However, Naples and Prato did not need enforcers as much as they had in years past. The FBI also investigated Naples for cocaine distribution in the mid-1980s, but nothing appears to have come of the case. There was no one to oppose Naples and Prato, and the only hits from now on would be internal family affairs. Mahoning County was relatively quiet for a time, but the stone-cold gangsters who inhabited the toughest rust belt county in America were not done wreaking havoc yet.

ERIE

The Pittsburgh family also wasn't done expanding. LaRocca and Genovese had Youngstown under their thumbs, but they were also casting greedy eyes up to Erie, Pennsylvania. Erie had been a traditional stronghold of the Buffalo mafia family, but prosecutions and age had diminished their control. According to the Pennsylvania Crime Commission, the Pittsburgh family filled the vacuum peacefully, and by the late 1980s, the main gambling operators in Erie were all laying off bets to Pittsburgh family bookies.[147]

4

"NO LEGS" OVER WEST VIRGINIA

I was dancing on a balance beam when I saw a guy come in…
and shoot my father.

—*Mattie David describing her father's murder*[148]

DELLERBA'S DEMISE

According to law enforcement authorities and the media, Italian immigrant and naturalized U.S. citizen Carla Dellerba was a madam for part of a prostitution ring that was located in Wheeling, West Virginia. The operation was allegedly under the aegis of gangster and notorious Pittsburgh mafia associate Paul "No Legs" Hankish. Dellerba was a minor player in the underworld and answered to her madam and overseer Aggie Toomer. Ronald Bris, a Hankish associate, and Hankish himself made money off the Toomer and Dellerba prostitution rings. Dellerba lived in a subdivided house in Canton, Ohio, across the border from her illegal business in West Virginia.

Dellerba had a long criminal history after she and her mother moved from northern Italy to the United States when Dellerba was a baby. They ended up in Pittsburgh, Pennsylvania, where Dellerba worked at an illegal gambling joint run by Pittsburgh mobster Frank Valenti when she was eighteen. Valenti later became her boyfriend and went on to head the rackets in

Bill Levis / Post-Gazette

Crime boss Paul Hankish leaves court after sentencing.

Paul "No Legs" Hankish in 1990. *Courtesy of the* Pittsburgh Post-Gazette.

Rochester, New York.[149] Dellerba was arrested as a prostitute for the first time in 1948. She had a few failed marriages after that until she found Pete Dellerba, who seems to have let her run her own life and vice versa. He had girlfriends on the side, and she had a boyfriend while married. In May 1974, Dellerba learned she had been indicted by a federal grand jury for sex trafficking across state lines.

Dellerba told Toomer she could not go to jail or be deported back to Italy. Dellerba was under a lot of stress and was trying to find a way out. Dellerba told her neighbors that she was done with prostitution and would try to cut a deal with the government and testify against her criminal superiors. Toomer's daughter and her boyfriend, the aforementioned Ronald Bris, did not trust that Dellerba would remain loyal to the organization if she faced significant jail time. Bris turned to Hankish for help. Hankish had the muscle to take care of it. Hankish hired unsuccessful boxer, gambling debt collector and leg breaker Ronald Asher to kill Dellerba.[150]

Hankish did not tell Asher anything about why Dellerba had to die but told him to work with Bris to get it done as quickly as possible. Hankish relayed the message by telling Asher that he had to "paint a house" for him. This was their code for committing a murder. Asher went to Canton to try to kill her on his own but kept missing her at her apartment. He finally went over with Bris and staked out the house with a car. Dellerba came home around 11:00 p.m., and Asher and Bris went to visit. According to Asher, Bris knocked on her door and introduced Asher as a friend. Dellerba trusted Bris and let him in with Asher. Bris and Dellerba talked for about fifteen minutes in the living room while the TV was on a low volume and Dellerba smoked. Dellerba went to the kitchen to put some coffee on for the group. Bris tried to pass Asher a pistol, but he waved him off, as he had a better idea of how to kill their target quietly. Dellerba returned, and Asher asked where the bathroom was located. Asher followed Dellerba, and as she reached in to turn the light on, he raised his arm and came down on her small five-foot-four-inch, 150-pound frame with tremendous force and broke her neck. She immediately flopped to the ground on her back and was still.

Asher knew she was dead, but Bris was unsure. They checked her pulse and found she had none, but Bris was still worried. As a result, they stabbed her three times and left the knife in her chest. They also stuffed a rag in her mouth and left that at the scene, too. The pair were careful not to touch much in the apartment and left little evidence of their presence, aside from the dead body, knife and rag.

Dellerba's husband found her a few hours later and seemed beside himself with grief. Dellerba was declared dead by the authorities, and despite the clear indications that Dellerba was murdered, the county coroner ruled her death a suicide. The coroner stated that she had stabbed herself to death, even though stabbing oneself deeply more than once is so painful that almost no person can do it three times. The idiotic, lazy or potentially corrupt ruling of suicide would stick for the next sixteen years.

In July 1990, Asher took the stand and testified against Hankish. He spoke about all the terrible things he had done for the local crime boss. He could not remember Dellerba's name but told the story anyway. The prosecution had made a deal with Asher that he would not be prosecuted for the hit if he gave up the person who ordered it.

On a ninety-degree day in Canton, Ohio, in late August 1990, a group of police, a funeral parlor owner and coroner staff watched as Carla Dellerba's body was dug up from her grave sixteen years after her untimely death. Asher's testimony had led Canton authorities to realize he was talking about their former resident when he detailed the murder from 1974. The authorities needed to figure out if Dellerba had been murdered. Her coffin was opened. According to an article written by the *Canton Rep* based on testimony from those who were there, Dellerba's body was still clothed in the pink dress and white pantyhose it had been buried in, and she also wore pearl earrings and a ring on her finger. The autopsy found the knife had pierced Dellerba's liver, heart, lung and stomach. The wound to the heart would have been fatal. Of course, the autopsy also found the neck injury that had ended Dellerba's life before the stabbing.

Asher had told the truth, and Dellerba's death was ruled a homicide. No one would officially pay the price for the murder due to Asher's immunity deal with prosecutors. However, the group that had ordered her death would fall from grace spectacularly. Maybe Carla Dellerba was avenged after all.[151]

Hankish's Rise

Today, Wheeling, West Virginia, is a small midwestern city with a population of about twenty-six thousand, but in 1900, it had about thirty-eight thousand residents. The city has seen a slow decline in population due to the gradual contraction of the coal and industrial jobs that once exclusively powered the area. In the 1960s, 1970s and 1980s, the town had a distinct blue collar feel, and enough industry was around that the city still had that character. It was a tough place to live, and Paul Hankish knew that ruling the city's underworld was a lot more complex and dangerous than most residents probably realized. The levels of criminal activity that occurred there were more appropriate for a much larger city, but Wheeling was a special case and had been dominated by organized crime for many decades by the 1980s.

In the 1950s, Hankish started out as a bettor who transitioned to the role of a bookie. Hankish was of Lebanese descent and grew up poor. His home life was anything but stable, and he took various low-paying jobs as a dishwasher or bartender in his younger years. His first big illegal operation was as a bookmaker in Bridgeport, Ohio, in 1957.[152]

In 1964, Paul Hankish was still a minor player in the underworld compared to his rival "Big Bill" Lias, the overweight Greek racketeer who had ruled Wheeling for decades. In the early 1960s, Hankish was busy getting in trouble for illegal gambling and burglarizing a supermarket.[153] It was all very small-time, and Hankish wanted more. Hankish had been paroled for an earlier conviction in 1963, which freed him up to continue his illegal pursuits.[154] Hankish was ostensibly employed as a used car salesman after his parole, a favored tactic of the Pittsburgh Borgata for hiding the origin of one's underworld income.[155]

In 1964, "Big Bill" Lias was concerned that Hankish was angling for his job atop the rackets in Wheeling. The young Hankish was setting up his own gambling empire and not asking for permission from Lias. Lias had gotten his start during Prohibition selling illegal liquor, and after the money from booze dried up, he started a numbers operation, opened several casinos, took a percentage of the profits from the prostitution business and bought the Wheeling Downs Racetrack. Lias was also an influence on local politicians in the Wheeling area. He had a lock on Wheeling until Hankish came along.[156]

On January 17, 1964, Hankish exited his house in suburban Warwood, a part of Wheeling, and entered his vehicle. He started the car, and then everything went to hell. Suddenly, he was trapped in a burning wreck. His car had exploded from a dynamite bomb that was connected to the ignition and seemingly placed in the front half of the car by the engine. The front end of the car was destroyed, the hood blown a block down the street, and the block's houses rocked by the shockwave of the explosion, incurring minor damages. Hankish repeatedly screamed at the police officers and firemen who rushed to the scene: "Get me out of here!" The bomb tore off one of his legs and partially severed the other. Hankish had to undergo a double amputation of what remained of both of his legs above the knee.

Initially, doctors gave him only a 50–50 chance of survival, but he pulled through and miraculously survived and thrived after the attempt on his life. Some say that in the delirium of those first moments after the bombing, he accused Lias of being behind the attack. Hankish would later deny this. The FBI was called in to help investigate, and they sent an explosives expert to examine the vehicle. All attempts to get Hankish to talk were in vain. The Wheeling police announced that Hankish had given them the names of three possible suspects, but Hankish had his lawyer publicly refute this and state that Hankish had given no one up to the police. Hankish was thinking of his underworld reputation even as he languished with no legs in a hospital room guarded by police.[157]

After Hankish's recovery, he ruled the rackets in Wheeling and used the remainder of the 1960s and early 1970s to cement and expand his territory. In the meantime, Lias's former empire was shrinking, and it was clear the failed hit had further isolated the old kingpin. Lias had always been more independent than Hankish. Hankish had close associations with multiple crime families and other independent operators, while Lias tried to keep his independence as much as he could, except for some ties to Cleveland mob figures. This tendency probably made Lias's profits large but did not give him close friends and allies during a trying time like the aftermath of the failed hit.

Hankish wanted Lias dead. Hankish went out of state to get help and hired Gambino family soldier Raymond Freda to take care of Lias. According to Freda, Hankish provided him and another Gambino soldier with two .38 pistols. The two men waited in a car outside of Lias's home for four days for him to come outside. He never left his house during that time. Hankish called the hit off once he learned that the FBI and police believed Lias was aware of the plot to kill him.[158] Lias died in 1970 of natural causes, and as a final act of revenge, Hankish allegedly had one of his associates steal the condolence book and cards from his funeral from the funeral home.[159]

In the 1970s, freed from Lias's malevolent presence, Hankish embarked on his lifetime project of leading the Wheeling underworld into what would become its golden era. No one would dare challenge him, and he was ready to make some real money. In the ensuing years, he would allegedly become involved in illegal gambling, prostitution, organized theft, extortion, loansharking, murders, drug trafficking, income tax evasion, pornography, food stamp fraud, health and human services fraud, student loan fraud, federal gun violations, arson, assault, domestic abuse, drug use, mail fraud and the alleged corruption of local officials. According to an associate, Hankish estimated his worth in the mid-1980s at about $3 million. It was not a bad payday for a child of a Lebanese immigrant who started out his gambling life as a dirt-poor bettor in one of the smaller cities of the United States.

Hankish's varied criminal career would see him involved in hijacking a truck filled with 1,456 cases of Stroh's beer in 1967, possessing a stolen painting called *The School Mistress* in 1969, stealing 259 cases of K-Mart clothing and 114 cases of Hershey candy bars in 1984 and cheating West Virginia out of $1,588 in sales taxes from his 1981 Mercedes Benz.[160] Hankish was also accused of having a team of professional shoplifters who would go to exclusive stores across the country to fill orders specified by Hankish. This activity resulted in a likely $6 million loss in expensive goods, such as crystal and jewelry.[161] In 1969, Hankish and thirteen others, including a former mayor and a former governor's aide, were indicted for being involved in a car theft ring that also stole women's dresses worth $27,000. The cars that were stolen were late-model luxury vehicles. The crew also hijacked tractor trailers.

Hankish sans beard. *Courtesy of the Pennsylvania State Archives.*

Hankish also used arson to get his way. Hankish ordered the firebombing of the Riverview Inn in Glenwood after the owner took out Hankish's slot machines. He often used Asher for these jobs, and Asher claimed in court that he had burned down three structures on Hankish's orders.[162]

These activities made money for Hankish but also created legal issues that he had to deal with through the 1960s and 1970s. Some of these crimes would even come back to haunt him as late as 1990. The attention and attempted prosecution of him for these crimes caused Hankish to become more cautious, and he eventually used payphones for business calls. He always kept a large amount of change on his person to make the calls and had a driver to chauffer him around to different payphones in order to avoid wiretaps. In the early 1980s, Hankish became obsessed with the Verilla case in Altoona, since Hankish had some gambling action in Blair County that had been outed by the grand jury's investigation. Hankish even ordered his associates to deliver local newspapers to him with updates on Verilla.[163]

CONNECTIONS

Hankish did not eat alone like Lias did and was described by the Pennsylvania Crime Commission as a mafia associate with a close relationship to Michael Genovese.[164] According to former FBI agent Roger Greenbank, Hankish would regularly travel to Orsini's Restaurant in Bridgeville, Pennsylvania, near Pittsburgh to pay a portion of his profits to Pecora, Porter or Zottola over the years. Hankish was often cited as an independent operator in historical media articles. The Orsini Restaurant meetings show that he answered to the Borgata just like every other big player in the region.[165]

Agents tracked Hankish as he had meetings with Pittsburgh mob members and traveled to the city multiple times. William "Eggy" Prosdocimo, the mafia-connected drug dealer and government witness, testified that Hankish had met Porter at Orsini's Restaurant to talk business. In addition, Porter, Hankish and Prosdocimo were all in the drug trade in the tristate area.[166] Hankish made Little Joey Naples the godfather of one of his children. Hankish also engaged in the sports bookmaking business with Naples and even gave him an allegedly stolen Mercedes Benz in or around 1981.[167] According to one source, Hankish was also allied with Pittsburgh mob heavyweight Kelly Mannarino and Pittsburgh mob drug dealer Joey Rosa. Mannarino was the godfather of a third Hankish child. Hankish also had friends in New York's Gambino family.

Raymond Freda and Joseph Covello were soldiers in that very powerful family and seemed to value their alliance with the Wheeling racketeer. Hankish's organization laid off bets to Covello, and Hankish allegedly did a favor for Covello and Freda by having a suspected informant killed in the 1960s. Covello was also the godfather of one of Hankish's children. Hankish also did business with the legendary North Jersey DeCavalcante crime family boss Sam "the Plumber" DeCavalcante. Hankish was deeply

Organized crime trial gives public look at the mob

By Janet Williams

The Pittsburgh Press

During three days of testimony, the jury of eight men and four women sitting in judgment on reputed La Cosa Nostra member Charles J. Porter and his codefendants have gotten quite an education on how the mob operates.

But jurors in the courtroom of U.S. District Judge Donald Ziegler have heard only limited testimony about how Porter, his brother William, or any of the other defendants fit into the organized crime family which prosecutors say exists in Western Pennsylvania.

That is expected to change tomorrow, when William "Eggy" Prosdocimo takes the witness stand to describe his role in two mob murders and his relationship with organized crime family members. Prosdocimo is serving life sentences for those murders.

Assistant U.S. Attorneys Bruce Teitelbaum and Stephen R. Kaufman hinted at what Prosdocimo's testimony promises Friday during a

'Eggy' Prosdocimo
Mob was his route up

Prosdocimo chose crime at early age

"Eggy" Prosdocimo. *As printed in the* Pittsburgh Post-Gazette.

interconnected with the mob and must have been making them money, since they mostly left him alone and appeared to trust him with some sensitive matters, including a murder.

In addition, Pennsylvania State Police intercepted a November 1988 phone call from Frank P. Unis Jr. of Aliquippa, a Pittsburgh mafia associate, to Hankish at a Wheeling restaurant. They had a cryptic conversation and discussed gambling line information.[168] Alfred Corbo, an alleged leading mafia associate in Altoona after Verilla's arrest in 1984, was also linked to Hankish's illegal gambling enterprise. According to the Pennsylvania Crime Commission, Hankish also laid off bets to Pittsburgh mafia associate Salvatore Williams's gambling operation.

Hankish's ties to the DeCavalcante family became stronger when independent drug importers with no organized crime protection shipped a large load of marijuana through Atlantic City, New Jersey, in 1983 and sent it on to Michigan. The Gambino family found out the contraband had crossed what they perceived as their turf and demanded a piece of the action from William Sundel and Victor Lubiejewski. Sundel and Lubiejewski were afraid the Gambinos would kill them, so Sundel reached out to Hankish for help. Hankish told Sundel to talk to an imprisoned Gambino soldier and convince him to say that the marijuana was a part of his criminal operations.

The jailed mobster agreed to state that he was a part of the deal from the beginning. Hankish then looped in Sam the Plumber to negotiate with the Gambino hierarchy. Sundel and Lubiejewski were ordered to pay $200,000, and the problem was solved.

After Hankish's help with his issue, Sundel started to use the Hankish network to bet on sports. Sundel bet the astounding sum of $350,000 to $400,000 every month with Hankish. He inevitably fell behind on his payments, and Hankish decided to visit the shady importer up at his Portsmouth, Rhode Island office. Hankish and two goons walked into Sundel's office while he was talking to a business associate. The associate was told to leave while Hankish brandished a handgun. One of Hankish's goons grabbed Sundel by the neck and bashed his head into different parts of the wall repeatedly. A contractor who later came by the office to fix the damage stated in court that it looked like Sundel's head had been used as a "stud finder."[169] Sundel, bloodied and desperate, ran into another office and started to load a pistol. Hankish followed him and pointed his handgun at his head. Sundel thought he was going to die, but everyone calmed down and a payment plan was discussed and adhered to by Sundel, who had managed to escape mafia-style retribution for the second time in the 1980s.[170]

INCOME SOURCES

Hankish's empire was built on illegal gambling. Illegal gambling was the bedrock of every one of the Pittsburgh mob's crews. The gambling profits were then invested from that staple to expand into legitimate business, drug trafficking or another illegal endeavor. Hankish's big moneymakers were bets on college and professional football games. Hankish and his associates also took bets on horse races. According to prosecutors at the time, Hankish's most famous gambling customer was Art Rooney, the founder of the Pittsburgh Steelers football team. Rooney allegedly bet hundreds of thousands with a Hankish-connected bookmaker on horse races. It was specifically stated that Rooney did not bet on sports, especially not football. The Rooney family denied that he ever bet with Hankish, but it was well known that Rooney was a habitual horse race bettor. Rooney died before any of these statements were made as trials proceeded against Hankish and his men.

A good example of how the Hankish organization's gambling apparatus worked is the story of Gerald "Snookie" Walls. Walls was a Hankish-affiliated bookie who took sports bets at his two bars in Uniontown in Fayette County starting in the fall of 1977. He made $1,800 a week at first and eventually $130,000 a week after only a few months. Walls kept one-third of the profits; another third went to Jimmy Griffin, who was the Hankish organization's intermediary; and the last third went to Hankish's main lieutenant, Charles "Buddy" Jacovetty. Griffin recruited Walls for Hankish, and his operation was part of a planned territorial expansion into Fayette County. Jacovetty and Griffin were Hankish's guys in charge of Wheeling, and they were key members of his criminal enterprise across several states. Walls was stunned by how much money he made in such a brief time, but soon, someone would come along to throw a monkey wrench into the money machine.[171]

DEALING WITH PIKE

Melvin Pike was already in his sixties in the late 1970s. However, his age did not slow him down. Pike was a Uniontown-based enforcer and racketeer with close ties to Porter and Mannarino. Pike was no saint. Pike had only one conviction in 1948, when he pleaded guilty to assaulting Uniontown police chief Charles Malik, who died a year later from his injuries. Pike was charged in the death of Malik in 1950, but the grand jury dismissed the charge. In 1973, he was charged with murder in the death of Uniontown boxer John Rodgers, who was stabbed during a fight at a Uniontown auto body shop. Rodgers was hospitalized but released and died three weeks later from complications. Pike was acquitted in 1974. One of Pike's wives, Lillian Pike, was found dead in a creek on November 24, 1965, of exposure near her Hopwood Township home. Her death was never solved. Pike reported her missing six days before her body was found under a bridge. She was last seen eleven days before her body was discovered.[172]

According to Walls, Pike would go out in the coal fields, steal expensive equipment and then offer the companies their equipment back for a fee of $12,000 to $15,000. Pike was also encroaching on Hankish's newly established gambling turf in southwestern Pennsylvania, possibly on behalf of the Mannarino group. According to the Department of Justice, Pike had also become aware that Hankish was using inside sports betting information to bet with Mannarino's group and was grossing $30,000 a week from them by cheating.[173] This was another reason to kill Pike. Despite the hierarchy and controls in place, internal conflict within the Pittsburgh family was commonplace and resulted in the aforementioned rivalry between Mannarino and Hankish and the rivalries between other factions, like those of Corbo and Verilla in Altoona. The structure of the mafia limited the rivalries somewhat, but the mob was tough on those who participated in it. Strength had to be shown at all times in the face of the rare external threat and the more numerous internal threats.

Walls stated seven Uniontown businessmen donated $5,000 apiece to hire a hit man to kill Pike. Hankish, Jacovetty, Griffin, Walls and Theodore Tsoras went to a meeting and asked Walls about his recent lackluster profits. Walls stated that Pike was the cause, and Hankish's leadership team decided without delay to kill Pike. Griffin hired Robert "the Codfish" Bricker to take Pike down. Walls's actions were made worse by the fact that Pike was his mentor and friend in organized crime who had taught him about the structure of the Cosa Nostra in the area.[174]

Bricker, the hired hit man, was known as the "Codfish" due to his alleged cold-blooded nature and ability to hurt or kill his targets without thinking twice. According to testimony from his associates, he was a contract murderer, and he was good at it. Bricker allegedly killed at least seven people during his time working in organized crime circles. His first murder occurred on the day he was married, December 26, 1963. Bricker needed money for his honeymoon and called up an acquaintance from the county workhouse. Bricker asked the man if he could borrow money, but when they met up, Bricker simply robbed him of the $500 he had on him, shot him twice in the chest, ran him over and then dragged him with his car as he screamed for about three hundred yards. Bricker pleaded guilty to the murder and was sentenced to life in prison but was let out after ten years. In 1974, the governor of Pennsylvania released him on lifetime parole based on the recommendation of the Pennsylvania Pardons Board, which noted his attainment of a high school and associate college degree while in prison. The board wrote, "If this man is released, he will become a useful member of society." They were wrong. The same year he was released, Bricker allegedly killed Raymond Mitchell and buried him behind his own house. The grave was not found until years later, and Bricker was never charged in the killing.[175]

According to Pike's daughter, who was ten years old at the time, Pike had detected people following him as he took her to her gymnastics class on April 17, 1978, in Canton Township. On April 19, Pike took her to class again. Pike was armed with a .38 pistol. Pike, despite his odious reputation, apparently loved his daughter deeply and had five keychain pictures of her on his keys that day. Pike's daughter was doing a routine on the balance beam, an attentive Pike watching, when Bricker, clad in a blue hooded sweatshirt, blue jeans and a ski mask, shot her father three times with a shotgun at close range in front of her. Bricker hit his target in the left arm, left shoulder blade and lower right back, near his waist. Pike died of a massive hemorrhage in his lungs.[176] As mentioned, Pike had powerful friends, and Bricker was tough, but he did not have the mob hierarchy behind him.

At 12:20 a.m. on December 10, 1980, Bricker was at his North Side home in Pittsburgh, sitting on the couch with his wife and child. Two shots were fired through the front living room window. They pierced the early morning calm, and suddenly, Bricker was bleeding out of his face and scurrying for his life. He ran from the window and crouched down in front of the door to hide. The shooter opened the unlocked storm door and looked through a window in the main door. He apparently saw Bricker cowering at the bottom of the door, because he stepped back and fired another six shots in the lower half of the door.

Robert "the Codfish" Bricker. *Courtesy of the* Pittsburgh Post-Gazette.

All of them missed, and the shooter ran from the scene. Police found seven spent .32 automatic shell casings on Bricker's porch. The attempted murder was unsolved for many years until a clue surfaced in a trial about ten years later.

A government witness testified that Porter told him that he was the shooter: "I shot him with a clean shot in the face, and he didn't die." Bricker was not involved in any more murders after the attempt on his life; although, he did unsuccessfully try to go after Porter for the shooting.[177] Porter denied shooting Bricker in federal court.

DRUGS

The drama did not end with the fallout from Bricker and Pike. The drug business was beckoning to Hankish to fill in the dropping gambling revenue he was experiencing due to the loss of some of his blue-collar customer base. The same economic trend that was affecting Youngstown, Pittsburgh and all the other tristate area cities was hitting Wheeling, too. In the 1980s and into the 1990s, West Virginia's economic powerhouses of coal, industry and steel experienced job losses.[178] The drugs kept profits up for a while, but as we have seen, the costs of the business were often far too high.

In 1981, Hankish started a drug ring that would eventually supply half the cocaine and marijuana in the greater Wheeling area. The enterprise would end up making Hankish's crew an estimated $925,000 in profit. However, the 1980s drug effort was preceded by a particularly heinous heroin importation scheme in the 1970s. Drug dealer Martin Trowery, serving a fifty-year sentence for his crimes, testified that he transported between twelve and sixteen kilos of heroin to Wheeling for Hankish from Pittsburgh. Trowery testified that the heroin came from Vietnam and was imported with the bodies of dead American soldiers returning home from the war. Trowery led this operation from about 1967 to 1970. Hankish was also involved with the Pittsburgh mob–connected Prosdocimo drug ring that resulted in several murders and a lot of media coverage that is the focus of chapter 5 of this book.

Hankish's new drug scheme was dependent on John Perrone, a Florida hairdresser whom Hankish had met while Hankish was at his condominium in the sunshine state. Perrone delivered drug money for Hankish and stored and diluted cocaine for him.[179] Hankish also conducted business with drug dealers Larry and Norman Farber and John Spagnoli, who sold the Florida cocaine. Farber was paying a percentage of his profits to Porter as part of the underboss's drug tax. The Farbers and Spagnoli were prosecuted for millions of dollars in drug sales in Pennsylvania and other locations.

According to associates, the drug trade started to corrupt Hankish, and he used what he sold sometimes. James Byrum, a former assistant county prosecutor, stated that Hankish sold him cocaine personally instead of acting through an intermediary. A concrete company executive and his former girlfriend also testified that they used cocaine with Byrum and Hankish in 1986 in the parking lot and bathrooms of a Wheeling nightclub. An associate purified the cocaine for Hankish and received between three and five grams a week for his trouble and reported going on double dates with Hankish and women who were not their wives.

In fact, Patricia Hankish, Hankish's wife, had found out about his extramarital affairs in the early 1980s and visited with a divorce attorney. She told Hankish she wanted a divorce, and he became enraged and choked her until she almost passed out. He told her there would be no divorce. However, he finally lived in a separate house from her by 1986.[180] Patricia was too afraid to go back to a lawyer, as she feared Hankish would hurt her or the lawyer if she tried. The bad family news was followed by a bad business development: Perrone, unknown to Hankish, was arrested in 1988 and started to cooperate with the government against Hankish's organization for a period of two years.

HANKISH'S EMPIRE FALLS

A three-year investigation by the FBI, IRS, West Virginia State Police and the Wheeling Police Department was already underway, with assistance provided by Florida law enforcement and the Bureau of Alcohol, Tobacco and Firearms.[181] The federal government was going to try to bring Hankish down by utilizing the Racketeer Influenced and Corrupt Organizations Act (RICO). No murder was too old and no allegation too small. Law enforcement wanted Hankish put away for good.

The gambling enterprise dominos started to fall on December 20, 1987, when gambling houses in Wheeling were raided by federal, state and local authorities. Gambling had been a cash cow for Hankish and his organization, and he had made an estimated $5 million from gambling in northern West Virginia and southwestern Pennsylvania alone. The raid seized money, records and gaming devices and included raids on Jacovetty's and Hankish's homes. It was the beginning of the end, even though no one was arrested that day.[182] Hankish had allegedly considered bombing the cars of U.S. attorney William Kolibash and an FBI agent to end their investigation of him, but he apparently thought better of it.

In October 1989, it all came crashing down. The arrests were not unexpected, given the raids two years before, but this operation was the actual death knell of organized crime in Wheeling. Hankish turned himself in to the U.S. marshals in Miami, Florida. Jacovetty was not arrested due to heart problems that caused him to be in a hospital in Wheeling. Tsoras was the only one who did not make his $50,000 bail, so he was stuck in prison for the time being. Eleven people in total were indicted on a crushing total of 218 counts.[183] The entire history of Hankish's operation was now out in the open for everyone to see. The indictment was shocking and comprehensive. Overnight, the organized rackets in Wheeling dried up and never returned. Criminals still existed in the area, but there was no successor to Hankish, and Wheeling had gotten rid of its mob cancer for good.

The trial started in June 1990, and Hankish chose a bench trial over a jury trial. He was betting on the opinion of one judge rather than rely on a jury of his peers. Asher, Walls and a third man testified against him. In the meantime, Jacovetty and many others took plea deals that involved them copping to charges that did not include the multiple murders in the indictment. A brief bit of unexpected theater occurred in court when the silver-haired, blind and ancient Sam "the Plumber" DeCavalcante showed up to testify as requested by the court. He didn't give up anything about

Hankish and only commented that he knew him and that they had shared some drinks. He then told the judge, "Good luck."[184]

Hankish had one weakness, even though he had treated her terribly during their marriage. His wife, Patricia, was charged in the case and faced considerable time in prison. Her lawyer argued that she was guilty only of being Hankish's wife, but the government disagreed. Hankish agreed to plead guilty to numerous charges if the government would not use the mandatory sentencing guidelines and drop the murder counts. He also wanted some of Patricia's charges dropped. The government did as he asked, and Patricia faced only three mail fraud charges. She was acquitted of those and was free to go. On October 25, 1990, Hankish pleaded guilty and received thirty-three and a half years in prison and a $72,500 fine for racketeering, gambling and drug trafficking.[185] The sentence meant Hankish would die in prison. Luckily for him, he was sent to the Federal Correctional Institution in Morgantown, West Virginia, since the facility had accommodations for inmates in wheelchairs. Hankish would be able to spend his last years in his home state.[186] Hankish died in prison in 1998.[187]

DRUGS

Money, Power and Peril

We have successfully severed the head from the body of the Cosa Nostra in western Pennsylvania.

—*U.S. attorney Thomas W. Corbett Jr.*[188]

THE OLD NEIGHBORHOOD

Larimer was a small corner of the mostly Italian neighborhood of East Liberty. There is only one Italian business left in Larimer today, a sausage shop called Henry Grasso Company Incorporated at 716 Larimer Avenue. The Grasso sausage shop opened when Larimer was still Pittsburgh's Little Italy. At the time, gangsters mingled with residents on the streets, and Mike Genovese hung out with his associates at the corner of Meadow Street and Larimer Avenue.[189] Actor Frank DiLeo, who played Tuddy Cicero in *Goodfellas*, hailed from Larimer. The mean streets of Larimer were an anvil that helped forge the tough guys who led Genovese's family. That same family would be sent down the road to eventual extinction by some of the ex-Larimer boys' adoption of drugs as a major income stream for the Borgata and the inclusion of men who were not from the old neighborhood in the trade.

Good Money, Bad Business

The Pittsburgh family started to get involved in drugs in a major way during the cocaine craze of the 1980s, when family members and associates could invest their plentiful illegal gambling profits into the new drug business. Business was booming, and the family ended up distributing thousands of kilos of cocaine during the 1980s and taking a piece of the action from drug deals made by other groups as part of Porter's drug tax. Genovese's Borgata became the largest drug supplier, profiteer and law enforcement target in the tristate area. The drugs came from various places through multiple rings but generally originated in Colombia and Florida.

Golden Goes Down

The first domino to fall was Gary Golden's cocaine and marijuana operation. Golden was a tight-lipped mafia associate and cousin to made member Sonny Ciancutti of the New Kensington crew. The scale of Golden's supply was truly enormous, as authorities once seized seven tons of marijuana with a street value of $7 million in 1981 from a home and warehouse connected to the Golden drug ring.[190] Golden also dealt in cocaine and hid his money in real estate transactions.[191] Golden and his ring were taken down in November 1982, when Golden bought $46,000 worth of cocaine from an undercover FBI agent. Fourteen people were arrested, and Golden was sentenced to twenty-five years in federal prison. Prosecutors attempted to get Golden to cooperate with authorities, but he refused.[192] However, seven members of his ring did cooperate, and his case exemplified the new reality that mafia members and associates may become government witnesses to avoid steep drug sentences.

Eggy's Betrayal

William "Eggy" Prosdocimo, a thirty-eight-year-old drug dealer and high school dropout from Squirrel Hill, also led his own mob-connected drug gang. The tall and muscular Prosdocimo enjoyed fighting and worked as an enforcer for then–mob associates Charles Porter and Eugene Gesuale.[193] He grabbed Porter's attention when he robbed some mob-connected drug dealers. Prosdocimo was eighteen when Gesuale and Porter brought him into the fringes of the mafia and started him out as a loanshark loan collector who would beat people up when they couldn't pay. Prosdocimo once remarked that it was "something like a paper route."[194] Prosdocimo graduated to lead his own cocaine ring and even fought a war against a splinter faction that terrorized Squirrel Hill in the 1970s. In 1980, Prosdocimo claimed he bribed a state judge to get one of his drug dealers off.[195] Prosdocimo was also the part-owner of a private club in East Liberty called the United Italian Republican Club.[196] Prosdocimo admitted that he once stuck multiple tarantula spiders down the pants of his landlord when he attempted to raise the rent on Prosdocimo's bar. Prosdocimo's star seemed to be rising in the underworld.

Prosdocimo's network started to unravel in June 1979. Twenty-eight-year-old Gary "Stretch" DeStefano was described as an affable man, an unemployed Vietnam veteran and a frequent traveler to Florida. Around midnight, DeStefano met his friend and Hankish crew associate Gerald "Snooky" Walls at the popular Butchie's After-Hours Club in Market Square in Pittsburgh. DeStefano left the club, telling Walls he would be right back. He never came back, and word later filtered through the club that the police were outside. In a parking lot across the street, DeStefano was lying dead under a white sheet, one .22-caliber bullet wound above his left eye.[197]

DeStefano, from Westmoreland County, had gotten involved in the drug business with Walls under Hankish. Hankish hired a hit man to murder Walls, and Prosdocimo helped set the hit up. Unfortunately for DeStefano, he was killed instead. The murder brought a lot of heat on Prosdocimo's group, since the police immediately recognized the signs of a professional hit. Walls threatened to kill Prosdocimo for DeStefano's death, but Prosdocimo ran to Porter for protection and Porter showed up at Walls's Uniontown residence with a group of thugs to tell Walls to back off.[198]

Thomas Sacco was another member of Prosdocimo's crew until Prosdocimo learned that he was reportedly a police informant. During the early morning hours of September 25, 1979, Sacco was outside a Market Square club with a few friends when a hooded man approached and shot him once in the neck and once in the left shoulder with a .38-caliber handgun and then fled. Sacco was killed. He had a troubled history and was arrested multiple times for a multitude of offenses. Sacco even had a brush with citywide infamy when he and two other men beat up Pittsburgh Steelers linebacker Jack Lambert in a downtown disco in 1978. According to some witnesses, Sacco yelled, "Come on, Bob," at the gunman before he opened fire.[199] This illustrated that Sacco possibly recognized the hit man.

Man Knew Killer, Police Believe

(Continued from Page 1)

Valenta said witnesses' accounts of the shooting conflicted, especially as to the direction the assailant took when he fled.

But, Valenta said, "We believe he (Sacco) must have known him. That's the direction the investigation is going now." Valenta did not say why the assailant is believed to have been known by Sacco and he said police currently have no suspects.

But other police sources said Sacco called out, "Come on, Bob (or Bobbie)," just before the shots were fired.

Sacco's killing is not believed to have been in gangland style because, police said, he was more of a "cheap hood" than a gangster figure.

He was also identified as one of three men who beat up Pittsburgh Steelers linebacker Jack Lambert in a Downtown disco last summer.

Sacco had a history of nine arrests in the last 12 years for offenses including drug violations, assault and battery,

THOMAS A. SACCO

armed robbery, terroristic threats, theft by receiving stolen property and parole violation.

Sacco was the second person shot to death in the Market Square area in the past few months. A Monessen man, Gary DeStafano, was found dead in a parking lot at Third and Market streets on June 14.

There, Jennings said, the sheet rope to bars cellblock wall and threw the Forbes Avenue.

"They must have done this utes," Jennings said, "be cellblock is under nearly con by the guards. These professionals."

Authorities said that Boat was seen by a parking lot when he fell on his back from was spied leaving the Carlton tel. He disappeared in the Robert Morris College.

Boatwright was convicted gravated assault charge awaiting sentencing, and Kar be tried for a $1,000 rob Wilkinsburg drugstore. He w June 15 after a high-speed

Bryant, a suspected mem "shot-and-beer gang," is accu eral robberies of taverns. Sir injured his arm in the escap was scheduled for trial in Southside bank robbery and a woman in her home as he f

Thomas Sacco. *As printed in the* Pittsburgh Post-Gazette.

Sacco was allegedly set up for the hit by notorious contract killer Robert "the Codfish" Bricker, who had also allegedly been involved in DeStefano's killing.[200] Bricker and Prosdocimo were arrested in 1980 for the death of DeStefano and Sacco. Bricker received the death penalty at the time for the Sacco murder but was acquitted of the DeStefano hit. Prosdocimo received life imprisonment for the DeStefano hit.[201] The sentencing of a minor mob associate in the equivalent of the crime family's draft team may seem of minor import. However, Prosdocimo's ties to Porter before he was in the family's hierarchy would make Prosdocimo a dangerous government witness in just a few years. Prosdocimo agreed to testify in any trials he might be needed for after his life sentence was handed down.

NICK THE BLADE

The next drug ring had a very strong connection to the mob's central players. Eugene "Nick the Blade" Gesuale, the infamous leader of the ring, became the symbol of the Pittsburgh mob's degeneracy in the 1980s. Gesuale was a six-foot-four-inch-tall, 250-pound high school dropout from East Liberty who, according to the FBI, ran a mob-connected club in the East Liberty neighborhood in 1966 that was owned by Mike Genovese. Gesuale, like

EUGENE A. GESUALE
Charged after Downtown brawl.

Eugene "Nick the Blade"
Gesuale. *As printed in the*
Pittsburgh Post-Gazette.

Genovese, enjoyed boxing, and there is even an old news article from 1953 that shows him boxing with another kid in the East End.[202] He was also a trained hairdresser by trade.[203] Gesuale had earned his moniker "Nick the Blade" from being proficient with a knife during altercations in the 1970s and even had the initials "NTB" monogrammed on some of his clothes, including his underwear.

Gesuale was a mafia entrepreneur with underworld businesses in illegal gambling clubs in Pittsburgh, a prostitution ring sanctioned by the New York crime families in Manhattan's Little Italy, a loansharking business and various drug-related endeavors.[204] Gesuale associate Paul Mazzei supplied gangster and government witness Henry Hill with Gesuale's drugs as the "Pittsburgh connection" made famous in the Scorsese movie *Goodfellas*.[205] Gesuale was also the source of some of Gary Golden's drugs. Gesuale operated his illegal businesses from the Beacon Club in Squirrel Hill and ran the loansharking business out of the club with Porter.[206] According to the FBI, Sonny Ciancutti was also a partner in the club.[207]

Gesuale was also described by law enforcement as crude, violent and reckless. A former FBI agent related that he witnessed Gesuale urinating off a balcony while snorting cocaine during a surveillance.[208] Gesuale was also flashy and bought the best clothes, most expensive cars and a penthouse apartment. Despite Gesuale's bad reputation with law enforcement, the Pittsburgh mob's hierarchy loved him, and he was a close associate of both Mike Genovese and Charles Porter. His antics may not have been ideal for secrecy purposes, but Gesuale made them money and knew how to keep his mouth shut, and that was all that was needed in the Pittsburgh mob of the 1980s.

Gesuale was arrested thirteen times between 1959 and 1981, including for allegedly being involved in a Lebanese heroin import scheme, but he was never convicted, except once on a shoplifting charge. According to a Pennsylvania judge, Gesuale was not held accountable because the witnesses would never testify.[209] In 1981, Gesuale attempted to run over a man who had lodged assault charges against him. After he missed with his car, Gesuale

Porter (*right*), Gesuale (*left*) and Robert Fitz of the Pagans Motorcycle Club (*center*) discuss the drug business. *FBI photograph.*

got out and attacked the man with a knife before firing a gun at the victim and threatening to kill him if he did not drop the charges. The man refused to testify against Gesuale.[210]

Gesuale got in big trouble with Genovese and Mannarino in 1977, when he and an associate robbed a courier who was transporting drugs and gold for a New York crime family. Porter stepped in to mediate the dispute and calmed things down with the Pittsburgh hierarchy. Porter was also able to avoid conflict between New York and Pittsburgh. Porter then mediated a dispute over $26,000 owed to Gesuale from a leader of the Pagans motorcycle gang who was distributing Gesuale's drugs based on alleged orders from his superior in the gang. The Pagan representative and Gesuale met in Porter's kitchen for a half hour, and Porter ruled that the Pagans had to pay Gesuale what they owed. Porter was also receiving a piece of Gesuale's action at the time, so he was not necessarily a neutral arbiter. Gesuale's partnership with the Pagans was a lucrative one. In one instance, the Pagans' representative gave Gesuale $650,000 in stolen gems as collateral on a $28,000 debt he owed the wiseguy. Unfortunately for him, he was arrested in 1982, before he could pay his cocaine debt and get the gems back.[211]

THE MOLE

Gesuale and the mob also had a little help from an unexpected place to keep them one step ahead of the law. Twenty-something FBI secretary Jaqueline Wymard worked for the organized crime squad in Pittsburgh. As a result, she knew about many of the investigations of the local mafia. Wymard had met forty-something mob associate John Carrabba Jr. at a Shadyside bar in 1982 and dated him for the next three years. Carrabba used Wymard as an information source and asked her often, "What's the FBI doing today?" Carrabba was in fact close to both Porter and Gesuale, and Wymard had a wealth of information about both men.

Wymard gave information to Carrabba about wiretaps, investigations and government witnesses. She even told Carrabba about Paul Mazzei's cooperation, endangering his life. She also informed Carrabba about the contents of teletypes and memos from the primary agent on organized crime in Pittsburgh, Roger Greenbank, to his bosses and FBI headquarters in Washington, D.C. Carrabba even asked her to steal a statement from a government witness. She did, but she forced him to burn it once he read it. Her leaks led to the intimidation of grand jury witnesses, some of whom refused to testify. However, Wymard is lucky that none of her leaks led to the deaths of any informants. Wymard was sentenced to five years' probation and Carrabba to three years imprisonment after Wymard was confronted in July 1985, after the FBI figured out she was the likely mole.[212]

A SATELLITE DISH IN JAMAICA

Gesuale's luck ran out in January 1985, when the federal government indicted him and the key players from his drug ring. The case was started in 1983 as an IRS tax matter but then ballooned into a drug conspiracy investigation when the DEA and FBI joined in. A few of Gesuale's associates cooperated and testified before the grand jury and then later in open court. The money flowing in from cocaine, heroin, marijuana and Quaaludes, some of the drugs from as far away as Colombia and Panama, was too much for law enforcement not to notice. Law enforcement successfully arrested and convicted five of Gesuale's major coconspirators and seized what property they could find. These seizures included those of his apartment and a Jaguar vehicle he had bought a few months before.

However, according to law enforcement, Gesuale was tipped off by Wymard's information that the indictments were coming, and he fled to Jamaica. He disappeared for about a year and a half in the Caribbean, living off an estimated $1 million that he had stashed away. He was also in touch with his Pittsburgh mob associates back home via phone and in-person contact when some mob-connected guys occasionally came to visit to give him funds. Gesuale had to move several times when he was tipped off that the U.S. marshals were hot on his trail, even in Jamaica. Gesuale was eventually discovered due to his expensive tastes and love of basketball betting. Investigators realized there were only two satellite dishes on the island, and one of them belonged to Gesuale. Jamaican security guards captured Gesuale at an airport near Montego Bay while he met with an alleged Peruvian cocaine trafficker.[213]

Gesuale came back to face justice in 1986, and he was convicted and sentenced to forty-five years in prison. Prosecutors tried to get him to cooperate against the Cosa Nostra bosses in Pittsburgh, but Gesuale never cracked. Gesuale was released from prison in 2014 but was forbidden from living in his old city, since he had threatened various people who had prosecuted him. He came back from prison to an old 1980s Rolls-Royce he had left with his sister for safekeeping. Gesuale moved to Florida and died from a heart attack on July 29, 2016, at the Past Times Bar in Ormond Beach while sipping a glass of Pinot Grigio.[214]

The Mafia Pedigree

Gesuale was very close to the mafia's leadership, but the next drug ring was headed by a young man who was in his late twenties and early thirties during the 1980s and was basically what passed for mob royalty in Pittsburgh at the time. Joseph Rosa was the grandson of member Joseph Sica and the son of member Frank Rosa. Joey Rosa grew up in suburban Penn Hills while his forbears got their start on the rough streets near Larimer Avenue. Rosa got involved in crime when he was sixteen years old and outfitted his car with police lights. Rosa and his friends would pull over drug dealers, watch them run away and then steal their drugs. One score netted the junior criminals $20,000. Rosa also gambled habitually as a youth and cheated one of Mannarino's bookmakers out of thousands of dollars once. Sica brought Rosa to a meeting with Mannarino, where he berated the youngster for his transgression and then gave him some Steelers tickets before he left. Rosa never gambled again.

One of Rosa's early mentors in the underworld was Louis Raucci, who helped keep the young mobster out of trouble and took a cut whenever he made a score. Raucci had been Rosa's father's protégé. Rosa's father gave him a black book with the names of all the people who owed him money just before he died. Rosa gave the book to Raucci and never saw it again. Before Rosa's father died, he helped Rosa start a jewelry store called JR Jewelers in downtown Pittsburgh's Clark building with some seed money. It seemed Rosa had a chance to become at least partially legitimate.

However, Rosa became bored of the business after a few years and decided to stage a fake robbery of the place and steal $300,000 worth of jewels for the insurance money. Rosa gave Porter a big piece of the action after he sold the jewels in Florida, too. Rosa claimed that this fake heist caught the attention of Mike Genovese, who called him to a meeting. Genovese congratulated Rosa at the meeting and stated that Rosa was now "one of them" and would not have to worry about anything anymore. Rosa assumed this meant that he was now a made member of the crime family, and some media articles refer to him as a member. However, in this author's opinion, Genovese's alleged statement is not an indication that Rosa was made on that day but that he had become an on-the-record associate of the family who could call on his superiors in Cosa Nostra for assistance with any issues he may have with other criminals. As stated earlier, the Pittsburgh crime family kept their membership rolls small and often treated their associates like made guys. Rosa's belief was not discouraged by the family, but he never went through the official induction ceremony with a burning saint card and pricked trigger finger that symbolized one's entrance into the secret society.[215]

As Porter gained prominence, Rosa delved deeper into the mob's business. Rosa started to deal cocaine with product from Florida traffickers Ramon Sosa and Irwin Levie, who were in two separate drug rings and obtained their supplies from Colombia. Porter received a $2,000 cut from every kilo Rosa sold. Rosa eventually bought and sold hundreds of kilos of cocaine with a large group of associates, just as Gesuale had before him. All was going well until Rosa became greedy and decided to rip Sosa off. Rosa grossly underpaid Sosa for a $400,000 shipment by placing $20 bills in the middle of the large cash payment in which all the bills were supposed to be $100 bills. Sosa did not find out about the $250,000 trick until Rosa left. Sosa was furious and sent his men to find Rosa in Pittsburgh. Sosa's men were not able to find Rosa, but Porter did. In a meeting attended by Raucci at Porter's house, he berated Rosa for his lack of foresight in maintaining what had been a lucrative relationship with a very stable cocaine importer.

However, according to Rosa, that did not stop Porter, Genovese and a few others from dividing Rosa's score among themselves as part of Rosa's tribute when he earned money under the auspices of the family.

According to federal authorities, Rosa sold cocaine from 1982 to 1986 and robbed other drug dealers on the orders of Porter and Raucci. During one meeting, Porter asked Rosa if he would like to rob a particularly profitable drug dealer but also indicated that Rosa may have to kill the victim. Porter suggested this by making the sign of a gun with his hand. Rosa declined the job. Rosa made an estimated $1.5 million during his short career with the mob.[216] Rosa's ring also included a former police officer and a cocaine-using state assistant district attorney who was alleged to have aided the ring by providing them with inside law enforcement information.[217]

DROZNEK'S DOWNFALL

Another associate of Rosa, Marvin "Babe" Droznek of Monroeville, was arrested in December 1986, after he sold a kilo of cocaine to undercover police officers.[218] Law enforcement was chipping away at the Rosa drug ring by reportedly monitoring the group's pagers and arresting members and turning them into government witnesses when they could. Droznek was almost unknown to investigators until around 1985, but he had been involved in crime for a while before then. Droznek started out as a robber and car thief before graduating to become a numbers writer. Droznek also functioned as a loan shark and enforcer for the mafia. Droznek was also acquainted personally with Porter. Droznek's legitimate business profile was also impressive and included the management of several restaurants and being named "man of the year" by the Monroeville Kiwanis Club.

Made member and son of the boss prior to LaRocca, Frank Amato Jr. was Droznek's sponsor in organized crime who oversaw his bookmaking activities and authorized Droznek to expand his enterprise by using the family's fearsome reputation on the street. Droznek became so close to Amato that Amato promised him he would sponsor his membership in Cosa Nostra if the books ever opened up. In court, Droznek detailed how Amato reported to Porter and how Droznek eventually had enough influence to go around Amato and report directly to Porter.

Droznek also revealed that one of western Pennsylvania's favorite pastimes, the game of bingo, had allegedly been corrupted by the Cosa Nostra. According to Droznek and some law enforcement figures, large and

Frank Amato Jr. (*far left*) and family. *Courtesy of the* Pittsburgh Post-Gazette.

small bingo games were being skimmed by organized crime figures who were even stealing from games whose proceeds were supposed to go to charity. The alleged organized crime beneficiaries of this bingo tribute scheme were Mannarino, Amato and Ciancutti. Imburgia's son-in-law's company also allegedly provided all the bingo supplies and strip tickets for a large bingo game that had suspiciously low amounts of donations given to the charities the games were supposed to be supporting.[219]

Droznek's criminal career ended in his early forties, when he agreed to wear a wire after his arrest and helped bring down the Rosa drug ring. Rosa was sentenced to ten years in prison and the twenty-something drug kingpin realized he did not want to be behind bars for so long. Rosa decided to cooperate, and law enforcement finally had a true insider to take down the powerful duo of Raucci and Porter.[220]

The Boss During the Investigation

Genovese and the other leadership figures clearly knew the investigation against the drug enterprises run by the family was ongoing, due to media reports, indictments, information from their mole in the FBI until she was arrested and the constant drumbeat of associates turning into government witnesses. In a rare FBI-recorded conversation of Genovese at LA Motors from July 1989, he spoke to Rosa's grandfather Joseph Sica about his grandson in a tone that seems sarcastic and possibly intended to take a jab at Sica in this author's opinion. Genovese stated, "Hey, Joe, it ain't your fault," and, "He's your grandson, you know what I mean? It ain't you. Ah, if you had control over him, it'd be different. But you had no control over him." Sica replied, "God, no." The tapes also caught Raucci talking to Genovese about how he would beat the IRS charges he anticipated in July 1989. Raucci addressed Genovese as "Boss" and then laid out a plan to account for his illegal income from 1985 to 1988.[221]

FINALE FOR PORTER AND RAUCCI

Porter and Raucci were arrested in April 1990 by federal task force authorities. Porter received a few courtesies from the FBI during the arrest—they cuffed him in the front and asked him if he wanted coffee while he was being processed—to play to the hierarchy and status of the men and possibly plant the seeds of cooperation. The Porter trial, as it came to be known in Pittsburgh, was the largest and most important organized crime prosecution that ever occurred in western Pennsylvania. No one knew it at the time, but the September 1990 trial was the beginning of the end of the mob in Pittsburgh. From 1985 to 1990, the mafia was as profitable as it had ever been in the area, and now, its two most active, intelligent, powerful and fearless members were in danger of long prison sentences.

Prosdocimo, Droznek, Rosa and many others were ready to testify against

Porter (*center top*) and his codefendants leaving federal court in 1990. *Courtesy of the* Pittsburgh Post-Gazette.

the left and right hands of Genovese himself. The drug trade had turned the very mob associates who were the likely future made members of the family into cooperating witnesses who would help bring the moneymaking and middle-management core of the family down. The witnesses did their job well. Porter testified in his own defense and simply rattled off that each charge was a lie, rather than explaining in detail why each charge or tale spun by the witnesses was wrong. It was not an impressive performance, and one wonders what he and his lawyer were thinking. The rest of the defense was a mob trial cliché of trying to undermine the credibility of the cooperating witnesses. It did not work.[222]

Porter (*right, looking into camera*) and his codefendants being loaded into a van after court. *Courtesy of the* Pittsburgh Post-Gazette.

Rosa received word of the reward for his cooperation in January 1991, when he was sentenced to less than four years in prison. He had already served most of that time, so he was scheduled for release into the witness protection program during the summer of 1991.[223] Porter and Raucci found out their fates after their federal racketeering convictions in October 1990. Porter received twenty-eight years in prison and Raucci got twenty-seven years. Porter said nothing at the sentencing when asked, and Raucci stated, "What can I say?"[224] Raucci died a few years later from natural causes while imprisoned. Porter still had a big part to play in the long-running drama that was the Pittsburgh crime family.

CASINO

Why do you hate me?[225]

—Henry Zottola to FBI agent Roger Greenbank

THE BRAINS OF THE OPERATION

Henry "Zebo" Zottola was likely a made member of the Pittsburgh mob and the guy who would take Porter's place as Michael Genovese's main conduit to the lower levels of the family and other families. Zottola seems to have come to the attention of the family in the 1970s. An early appearance in the media in 1972 connected Zottola to a postage stamp theft scheme involving tens of thousands of dollars in stamps.[226] The Pennsylvania Crime Commission stated Zottola engaged in numbers and sports betting, loansharking and funding drug transactions. Zottola became close with former underboss Joseph Pecora of West Virginia and even lived in that state for a time. Zottola reportedly watched over Pecora's interests in the panhandle and elsewhere while Pecora was in prison in the early 1980s. He was diplomatic, friendly and tough. The FBI reported that Zottola was one of the frequent visitors to Genovese's table at the Holiday House in 1985.[227]

Zottola was also one of the Pittsburgh members who had true business savvy and was often connected to or starting up different businesses. He was involved in J and Z Vending with Pecora in the late 1970s; was president of Rocca's Italian Foods, which had Raucci as an "employee";

A younger Henry Zottola. *Courtesy of an anonymous researcher.*

and was associated with the comically named Consigliere Corporation. This company was formed in late 1991 to run the Consigliere Restaurant on Forbes Avenue in Pittsburgh. Zottola also owned S and S Carpet Service Incorporated, which gained media attention when its ties to the mob were revealed after the company gained a contract to lay carpet and tile at the Pittsburgh Airport. Zottola was also involved with a games of chance rental company called Tidan Incorporated and allegedly had a stake in coal mining concerns in West Virginia. He was also the owner of the Oakmont Car Wash and once tried to start up a McDonald's restaurant franchise, but the business failed.

Zottola also reportedly had poker machines in Veterans of Foreign Wars and American Legion posts in New Castle, Pennsylvania. According to the FBI, in the mid-1990s, Zottola and another unnamed Pittsburgh mafia member or associate were busy forcing "small produce retailers" in the East Hills section of Pittsburgh to buy their produce and meat from suppliers who were favored by the mob. Prior to the 1990 trial, Zottola reported to Louis Raucci but was already handling management tasks for the boss himself, too.[228]

In 1990, Genovese's family was in trouble. The Porter trial had taken out the boss's middle management, along with numerous key associates. Post-Porter, Zottola was the perfect choice to be Genovese's representative to the lower echelons and other families as needed. He was polished, had the air of a businessman and dressed the part, and he was well respected. He was unfailingly polite like Porter but seemingly without the hot head that the old underboss was infamous for in his early years.[229] Zottola also already had strong connections to the family's associates in West Virginia from his Pecora days, had cultivated ties with the Youngstown crew when he became the conduit for the profits there to Genovese and was a very active member who never seemed to run out of ideas about how to make money. According to FBI informants, by 1995, Zottola was basically running the day-to-day affairs of the family for Genovese, despite the fact that John Bazzano Jr. was reportedly the new underboss of the family.

Zottola's next scheme had the potential to be very lucrative on its own. It also had the added benefit of being a potential conduit to launder millions in illegal gambling profits. Zottola wanted to lead the charge for the family to own a legal casino again for the first time since the Mannarinos had partially owned the Sans Souci in Cuba in the 1950s.

RINCON

The casino targeted for a takeover was the Rincon River Oaks Casino in Valley Center, California. The Rincon Indian Reservation is located thirty-five miles northeast of San Diego. The casino had been the pride of the small Rincon band of Luiseño Natives, but it already had a checkered history when Zottola and the Pittsburgh family decided to get involved. The Chicago family of La Cosa Nostra, one of the most powerful Borgatas in the United States at the time, also tried to take over the Rincon Casino and failed, with the conspirators getting jail time. The Chicago mobsters' case ended in 1993, and Zottola's plan started to gather steam only a year later in 1994. The tribe members in charge of the Rincon were once again reaching out urgently for investors for their defunct casino, and the wrong people came knocking for a second time. Pittsburgh family made member Pasquale Ferruccio was also involved with the plot and collaborated closely with the mob's contact within the tribe.[230]

The plot was well thought out and involved a front organization of alleged lawyers and doctors who wanted to invest and manage a casino. The Columbia Group was largely made up of investors from Pittsburgh organized crime and illegal gambling operatives from Ohio and Pennsylvania who wanted to start out by laundering $2.1 million in illegal gambling profits through the casino. The main "investors" were Zottola, Ferruccio, western Pennsylvania gambling kingpin and mob associate John "Duffy" Conley and Pittsburgh attorney Dennis Miller. Dominic Strollo, the brother of made Youngstown crew member Lenine Strollo, who played a minor part in the Cleveland-Pittsburgh mob war, also invested money in the casino on behalf of his organized crime sibling. Lenny Strollo was also involved in another ostensibly legal and pioneering gambling venture in the 1990s, when he invested in a hotel in Puerto Rico to further offshore and internet gambling businesses for the mob. The Columbia Group ruse would help get past the checks performed by the National Indian Gaming Commission for ties to organized crime.[231]

MEETING WITH MILANO

In February 1995, a special visitor came to the Cleveland area, where his family roots were strong. According to FBI files, the don of the small Los Angeles mafia family Peter Milano was in Cleveland to visit his blood relatives, reestablish business contacts with the remnants of the Cleveland mob and meet with Zottola about Rincon. The visit and pitch had been set up by trips to California prior to the February summit. William "Big Billy" D'Elia, the last remaining truly active member of the tattered remnants of the Bufalino family of northeastern Pennsylvania, was a Zottola ally and underworld diplomat who had met with Milano to help with the Rincon deal. Milano's family had claimed San Diego as their own, and the FBI thought that Zottola's meeting with Milano was to ask the don's permission to operate in his territory. It appears that John Bazzano Jr. and Lenny Strollo were also at the meeting in Aurora, Ohio. Approval was apparently given by Milano, and the project moved forward. Once again, as he did with Scarfo's visit to Pittsburgh, Genovese was not at the meeting. His need for secrecy knew no bounds.

Left: Henry Zottola (*left*), Lenine Strollo (*center*) and John Bazzano Jr. (*right*) stroll down a street in Aurora, Ohio, on the day they met Los Angeles don Peter Milano in February 1995. *FBI photograph.*

Right: Los Angeles boss Peter Milano (*left*) and an unidentified associate walk down the street in Aurora, Ohio, on the same day they had a meeting with representatives of the Pittsburgh family. *FBI photograph.*

THE CASINO OPENS

Back on the reservation, Ruth Calac, a member of the Rincon Tribal Council, apparently knew Ferruccio before Zottola's approach. She had vehemently and publicly denounced the Chicago mob for their attempt to take over the Rincon Casino and had even been part of the original pushback against them in the late 1980s and early 1990s. Calac forgot her scruples and her loyalty to her tribe when she accepted bribes in the form of a leased car and $15,000 from Ferruccio in order to look the other way and approve of the Columbia Group as an investor. She then tried to hide the true identities of the group once the bid was accepted.[232]

The casino had card games and bingo, but to become truly profitable it had to have video poker slot machines. However, there was a moratorium on any new tribal slot machines in California at the time. Also, the slot machines owned by the Columbia group were purchased in Las Vegas, Nevada, and were meant to go to South Carolina, where they were legal. Instead, the machines were diverted through Arizona to California and then to the Rincon Casino in 1995. A highly placed FBI source in the Pittsburgh mafia—more on him later—outlined the Rincon scheme to the FBI, and the FBI seized documents in another search warrant on a gaming company that showed Zottola trying to form the Columbia Group. According to the FBI, Zottola also had associates of his working at the casino and visited the site often.

The casino opened in April 1995 with four hundred video poker slot machines—until the local United States Attorney's Office filed against the casino for violating the California ban on new slot machines. The move worked, and the machines were taken from the casino after only one day of operation. The newly refurbished twenty-thousand-square-foot space now hosted only bingo and card games that were not nearly as profitable as the one-armed bandits. The casino closed in June 1996, and the Pittsburgh mob's attempt to create a moneymaking machine in Southern California died with it.

ZOTTOLA'S FALL

In April 1997, seventeen people were indicted by federal authorities on bribery, money laundering and fraud charges for the casino takeover. Zottola pleaded guilty to bribery and trying to obstruct the National Indian Gaming

Commission. Zottola was sentenced to one year of home detention and two years of probation in May 1998, due to his battle with a fatal cancer diagnosis. Assistant U.S. attorney Bruce Teitelbaum said, "No one wanted the guy to suffer and die in prison."[233] Zottola once asked Pittsburgh FBI agent Roger Greenbank why he hated him. Greenbank had responded that he was just doing his job. It appears that Zottola's businesslike demeanor and polished approach, as well as his polite manner when dealing with law enforcement, had gained him a certain amount of respect and sympathy from his government adversaries. Zottola's prosecution and death isolated Genovese even further, and the failure of the casino resulted in the family losing millions from their investment, much of which was simply kept by the tribe when the mobsters were kicked out. A major route to laundering the mob's money and making it appear legitimate had been closed. As of August 1998, Henry "Zebo" Zottola, the most active Pittsburgh Cosa Nostra member left at the time, was dead at the age of sixty-three, along with any hope of reviving the fortunes of the aging and battered Pittsburgh family.

7

MAYHEM IN YOUNGSTOWN

We'll take care of it.

—*Bernie Altshuler to Lenine Strollo after being asked to kill a prosecutor*[234]

LIVE BY THE GUN, DIE BY THE GUN

In August 1991, Little Joey Naples and the Pittsburgh family were the undisputed kings of the rackets in Youngstown, Ohio. His mentor and fellow Pittsburgh mafia member Jimmy Prato had died a few years before from natural causes, leaving Naples as the coleader of arguably the most lucrative satellite group in the Pittsburgh family. Little Joey had survived two mafia wars and multiple federal and state investigations and had worked hard to protect his multimillion-dollar illegal gambling business. His reputation in the underworld was at its height, and the other made guy he shared Youngstown with could not hold a candle to Naples's legend.

On the night of August 19, 1991, the fifty-eight-year-old Naples was inspecting a new home he was having built in rural Canfield, Ohio, when someone killed him with two shots to his chest and back. Emergency services were called at 8:07 p.m. Neighbors reported hearing two shots, then silence and then two or three more shots. Law enforcement's theory for this killing was that the hit man or hitmen had a rifle and were positioned in a nearby cornfield to take the crew leader out.[235] Empty shell casings were found in the field about twenty feet from Naples's body. The perch where the hit man had hidden himself consisted of cornstalks about six feet tall; it was the perfect place to ambush the cagey mobster who had avoided death so many times before.[236] The police found broken cornstalks and depressions in the corn where the killer or killers had hidden.[237]

The murder remains unsolved, but theories have been put forward. The first question to ask when a mafia murder occurs is: Who benefits from the victim being dead? In this case, Lenine Strollo, another made member of the Pittsburgh mafia and a longtime illegal gambling fixture in the Youngstown area, had the most to gain. Strollo was not technically under Naples but ruled over his own lucrative turf as coleader with him. Naples had the reputation and notoriety, while Strollo toiled in the shadows. Strollo reportedly hated Naples and viewed him as his main rival. Strollo even allegedly put it out on the street that Naples was an FBI informant, even though there was no evidence to suggest that was true.

Strollo ran the All-American Club and illegal casino in Campbell, Ohio, before the murder. The place had generated an astounding $20 million a year in estimated income for the Pittsburgh family and was the largest and most profitable illegal casino ever discovered in the United States. The casino featured poker and blackjack games and betting on the Pennsylvania and Ohio lottery numbers. The profits made by the casino were invested in drug trafficking, legitimate businesses and racketeering by the Pittsburgh mob.[238]

According to a confidential FBI informant, Strollo was worried that Naples would take over his gambling interests after Strollo was sent to prison for fourteen months in 1990. His conviction was based on the crimes he committed while running the casino, which included the bribery of local officials in Campbell, Ohio, to look the other way while the casino operated.[239] The FBI had bugged Strollo's headquarters at the Stardust Motel. Less than a year after Strollo went to jail, Naples was dead.

There is also a theory that an individual operating on their own killed Naples to impress Strollo and gain entrance into his good graces. This scenario is possible in

Lenine Strollo. *U.S. Marshals' photograph.*

organized crime, but the alleged killer was not murdered himself for allegedly performing an unsanctioned hit. As a result, the independent operator theory seems to be lacking, unless the alleged killer was impossible to get to once the family discovered his identity. Strollo vehemently denied any part in Naples's murder. Naples was a rare asset in the Pittsburgh family's ranks, and it seems foolish that they would kill him for anything but a profoundly serious violation. The sources are silent on any such reason.

In the end—and as a result of Naples's murder—Strollo learned that he would be the lone head of the rackets in the Youngstown area while he was living in a halfway house as he transitioned out of prison.[240] Charles Imburgia, the consigliere of the Pittsburgh family, ordered Strollo to a meeting in late 1991 with aforementioned made member Pasquale Ferruccio and told him the good news. It had taken a long time, but sixty-year-old Lenny Strollo was the local mafia kingpin at last with the blessing of the bosses in Pittsburgh.[241]

Lenny's Rise

According to the *Cleveland Scene* and the *Lancaster Gazette*, Lenny Strollo started out his criminal life when he was a teenager working at a Youngstown repair shop, washing windows and cleaning the place. The guys who ran the shop eventually taught Lenny how to fix the slot, pinball, vending and bowling machines that were in the mill workers' bars. Strollo's vending machine side job earned him a few hundred dollars a week, much more than he could have made in any legitimate nongambling job at the time. As Strollo grew up, he obtained his own machines and his own territory. However, as Strollo started to turn a profit, his competitors moved in to take some of the action. Strollo turned to Prato for help in the 1960s, and Prato agreed to protect his operation for a cut. Strollo's career was sidelined for a while when he was arrested in 1963 for counterfeiting ten dollar bills, and after many appeals, he finally went to prison in 1967.[242]

Strollo managed to survive the mafia war without getting killed or arrested and was not involved with any of the major federal drug and gambling cases that started to decimate the Pittsburgh mafia in the 1980s and culminated with the trial of Porter and Raucci in 1990. Strollo had his short stint in prison for the casino bust, but that hardly slowed him down. Strollo was finally made into the mafia in 1987, when he showed up to a meeting in a made member's basement, where Mike Genovese and other leading figures were present. Strollo was made in the traditional manner: he got his finger pricked and held a burning saint card in his hands while pledging that he would uphold the vow of silence about mafia business no matter what.[243] Naples was made at the same ceremony, and both men had been proposed for membership by Prato just before he died. Ciancutti and Porter were made at a ceremony in another basement the year before.

Porter and Henry "Zebo" Zottola were the conduits to Genovese from Youngstown, and all of Naples's business went through them until 1990.[244] In 1991, Porter was in jail and Naples was dead, so Zottola was Genovese's eyes, ears, mouth and cash collector in Youngstown to give Genovese some insulation from the very active and risky crew in eastern Ohio.[245]

STROLLO'S TEAM

Strollo's top lieutenants in the Youngstown area were Bernard "Bernie the Jew" Altshuler, Lawrence "Jeep" Garono and Ernie Biondillo. Strollo had worked with Altshuler since at least the 1970s, when they set up a gambling game together. Altshuler also worked at Strollo's All-American Club. Altshuler was destined to become Strollo's most trusted advisor and had deep ties with the drug dealers and illegal gambling operatives in Youngstown's Black criminal circles. Altshuler would allow Strollo to lean on this untapped criminal talent for the benefit of the Pittsburgh mafia in the 1990s. Altshuler had been arrested by the FBI on May 25, 1992, while attempting to break into

MOB RULE

MOB FROM PAGE C-8

exchange for protecting their rackets.

He denied the charge, but then, acting as his own attorney, testified in federal court that he had taken the money as part of a plan to trap the mobsters.

He was acquitted. A few years later, though, U.S. Tax Court ruled that he owed back taxes for accepting $108,000 in bribes. By then, Traficant had been elected to Congress. Last year he was re-elected to a seventh term, winning 91 percent of the vote.

Unorganized crime

Lately, public corruption scandals have overshadowed the city's usual preoccupation with mob activities. Dan Ryan, a radio talk show

Ernest Biondillo

Ernie Biondillo. *As printed in the* Pittsburgh Post-Gazette.

the United Carolina Bank in Charlotte, North Carolina, with the infamous Dinsio family of bank robbers. Altshuler was described as a "safecracker" in a media article after the incident.[246]

According to a *Pittsburgh Post-Gazette* article, Lawrence Garono was a longtime gambling operative, a sometime enforcer and a political corruption fixer. Garono ran the barbut dice games at a mafia-run bar called the Army-Navy Club and once remarked that a good way to get deadbeat gamblers to pay up was to put them in a bag and beat them with a baseball bat. Garono also reportedly used his cousin, who was a chief of detectives for Mahoning County, to raid illegal gambling operations that weren't approved by Strollo.

Ernie Biondillo was Naples's old protégé and was adept at the business of illegal gambling, political corruption and building alliances. Biondillo had also worked with Strollo at the All-American Club in Campbell. Biondillo was not a made man yet. According to an FBI informant, Naples had planned to give Biondillo day-to-day control of his rackets before he was killed.[247]

Altshuler's Ingenuity and Mafia Wannabees

Youngstown's economy had been in freefall since 1977, when Youngstown Sheet and Tube closed, and five thousand people lost their jobs. The rest of the 1980s in Youngstown were similar, as the rest of the steel industry collapsed during and after the Cleveland-Pittsburgh mafia war. By 1991, tens of thousands of people had lost their jobs, and many had left the city. The city's middle-class workers, homeowners and the businesses that depended on them, like stores, restaurants and bars, gradually disappeared. Youngstown's population dropped and became poorer, while crime and violence rose in the streets. Strollo's illegal gambling business was also losing some profit due to the lack of mill workers with money to feed his games of chance.[248]

Altshuler produced a solution that would partially fix this deficit. Altshuler proposed that he be allowed to use his underworld contacts in Black criminal circles to get drug dealers to gamble at Strollo's games. Drug dealers were some of the few people left in Youngstown who could afford to spend money on a luxury like gambling. Altshuler used two popular and influential drug dealers named Jeff Riddle and Lavance Turnage to lure their friends and associates into gambling with the Pittsburgh mafia.

Riddle would later brag to his friends that he would become the first Black man to get inducted into the mafia. This was unlikely given the ethnic requirements for made membership in Cosa Nostra, as Riddle, unlike Porter, did not even have a partial Italian heritage to lean on. However, Riddle was to become a highly valued and trusted mob associate and leader in Strollo's group. Strollo's mafia crew was still led by Italians, but its makeup was quickly becoming multiethnic as time wore on. Strollo's alliance with Black and Jewish criminals would also fill his need for muscle to remain dominant and respected in eastern Ohio.

In the meantime, Altshuler and Riddle ran craps games at Sharkey's Nightclub in Campbell, while the aforementioned former high school football star and college dropout Lavance Turnage hung around with another Altshuler associate and drug dealer named Antwan "Mo Man" Harris.[249]

Strollo's crew wasn't only popular with Black criminals in the 1990s. Law enforcement alleged that on July 17, 1994, James Quinn; Samuel Fossesca, of note for his participation in the Youngstown mafia war; and James Napolitano stole $1.6 million worth of jewels from the Headley-Whitney Museum in farm country in Kentucky. The heist was almost perfectly planned, and the thieves even stole the security system. The haul included a golden castle covered with diamonds and rubies, a gold mask and an abalone horse head studded with rubies. The men took over half of the treasure from the museum that hosted the masterworks of George Headley, a jewelry designer for Hollywood stars.[250] The heist was part of a $10 million crime spree the Youngstown area men undertook to impress the mafia and to pay tribute to gain acceptance by the Pittsburgh family.[251] According to the FBI, the jewels were unlikely to be recovered, as they had been broken up and sold by the time the men were brought to justice.

THE SHADOW GOVERNMENT

Strollo had several gambling enterprises in the city of Campbell, Ohio, near Youngstown. Campbell is a small town of about eight thousand residents that also had an industry-based economy until the economic destruction of the 1980s. Stunningly, Strollo held complete sway over the town's law enforcement. Strollo had the town's law director Michael Rich in his pocket. Rich helped Strollo corrupt other officials.

In one instance, Strollo wanted to make a sergeant by the name of Charlie Xenakis, who was friendly to the rackets, the next chief of the Campbell police. The process to pick a new chief was supposed to be based on the scores each applicant achieved on the civil service exam, and then the mayor would choose who the next chief was from the top two scores. Strollo asked Rich to corrupt the process so Strollo would get who he wanted. Rich rigged the test so that only Xenakis would pass, and the mayor had only one choice to make. Lawrence Garono and Dante Strollo, Lenny's older brother who had helped with the Rincon Casino scheme, also paid bribes to Xenakis to keep him motivated.

The effectiveness of the payoffs in Campbell could be seen during a traffic stop that could have been disastrous for Altshuler's and Riddle's team. Three associates of Riddle and Altshuler, including the aforementioned Mo Man Harris, were speeding and got pulled over by the Campbell police in 1996. Police found an AK-47 rifle, a .357 Magnum revolver and a 9-millimeter handgun. One of the men called Riddle for help. Riddle went over to the traffic stop and told the police officers that the guys were working for Altshuler. The cops let them go.

Strollo always kept himself at an arm's length from the direct criminal acts performed by his associates. He only worked through a few trusted people. Altshuler was his connection to the muscle and gambling in Black underworld circles, Garono and Dante helped him with his illegal gambling enterprises and Biondillo handled Naples's old illegal businesses out of his headquarters at Youngstown United Music, officially listed as a vending machine company, with a burgeoning crew of his own.[252] This approach allowed Lenny to stay out of the law's reach for a while, and it was the normal modus operandi of the Pittsburgh mob's hierarchy.

Strollo had also corrupted Mahoning county prosecutor James Philomena, who had allegedly taken a piece of a $100,000 bribe from Strollo intermediary and disbarred attorney George Alexander in order to obtain leniency for Mo Man Harris, who faced a murder charge.[253] In another incident, Strollo related that he had given free lawn work to a judge to get a DUI dismissed for someone. In the end, Strollo, Altshuler, Riddle and Turnage decided to make a business out of fixing cases. The group would make an offer to fix a case for some of the local criminals and drug dealers and charge them a fee that the group would take a portion of for themselves. The rest of the money would be passed off to George Alexander or one of the other fixers to pay off the appropriate prosecutor or official. In short, it seemed that a significant part of the law enforcement and criminal justice establishment in and around Youngstown was working for the benefit of the mafia rather than the public.

According to Strollo, his reach went far beyond Pennsylvania. Strollo stated that he had helped an Ohio fireworks company owner get out of a conflict with Gambino boss John Gotti. The owner allegedly came to Strollo for help since Gotti wanted $300,000 from him for selling fireworks in New York without the Gambino family's permission. The Gambino family claimed they had a deal with the fireworks company for 10 percent of its New York profits. The owner feared getting hurt or killed during the dispute. Strollo said he quashed the Gambino demand after the owner paid him $100,000 to make the problem go away. The owner also paid Strollo about $25,000 a year for protection from politicians and other organized crime figures after this incident. The fireworks company denied this version of events but admitted that Strollo did extort money from the owner.[254]

The Problem with Biondillo

In the summer of 1995, Strollo attended the birthday party of Altshuler's wife and let himself relax among his business associates and friends. The party was a real gangland affair, with Biondillo, Henry Zottola, Garono and some lower-level gambling operatives in attendance. According to Strollo, all of them were drinking wine at the party when Biondillo started to talk about Strollo and stated, "Look, there he is; he thinks he's the boss. We just make him think he's the boss." Strollo heard the comment but ignored it in the moment. However, Zottola, Genovese's representative, spoke up immediately and got incredibly angry with Biondillo. Soon after this incident, Strollo started to receive reports that Biondillo was running unauthorized gambling games in Youngstown and that he had started to operate poker machines in Hillsville, Pennsylvania. Pasquale Ferruccio, an expert in gambling machines, was the source of the information about Biondillo's rogue machines. As a result, Strollo took the situation very seriously. Strollo confronted Biondillo about the poker machines directly, and Biondillo chose to lie to Strollo and tell him he did not know who the machines belonged to. Strollo was not getting any piece of the action generated by those machines. It seemed Biondillo was building his own war chest on the side. To make matters worse, Biondillo was also reportedly making statements about how he was "the new kid on the block."[255]

The next move by the "new kid on the block" came in the 1996 Mahoning County sheriff's race, the same race that had caught Congressman Jim

Traficant with his pants down accepting money from both the Cleveland and Pittsburgh mafia years before. Strollo had decided to support Phil Chance for sheriff and had donated and bribed him and his campaign directly through Garono and Charles O'Nesti. O'Nesti was a savvy political operative who was close to Congressman Traficant and became a bagman for Strollo.[256]

"The Center," which is what Biondillo's crew was called due to their location on Center Street in Youngstown, was busy making its own political moves. According to Strollo, Biondillo was backing two different candidates for sheriff with his money and was doing so without Strollo's approval by supporting the candidacy of the Youngstown police chief and that of Youngstown councilman James Pastore. It was a direct challenge to Strollo's dominance and his position as head of the Youngstown crew. Zottola stayed connected with both factions during this time, and he was the one who reportedly passed Strollo the intelligence about Biondillo's support of the police chief in the sheriff's race. Strollo's pick eventually won the sheriff's position.

At the same time, Strollo heard from one of his associates, who also did business with Biondillo, that he had overheard Biondillo say, "Well, just a matter of time—we'll get rid of him." Strollo acted nonchalant when he was told this, but privately, it made him angry and worried. If Biondillo was planning to kill him, he knew who the likely shooter would be. Mark Batcho was an up-and-comer in Biondillo's crew who functioned as Ernie's bodyguard. Batcho was described by Strollo as "somewhat of a nut." Batcho had once stabbed a guy for talking to his wife at a bar and attempted to blow up a friend's house after the friend allegedly damaged Batcho's mom's house.

In the meantime, Biondillo had beefed up his crew with two guys from Canada who had moved to the area. This development concerned Strollo greatly, as the Canadians decided to stick around and open a beauty shop in Youngstown. According to word on the street heard by Strollo, the men were allegedly relatives of Pasquale Ferruccio. Biondillo was also reportedly trying to get a made guy from Florida to move to Ohio to help him out.

Strollo had extensive conversations with Zottola about Biondillo's alleged reinforcements. Zottola was concerned after the remarks Biondillo made at the party in 1995 and all the other signs that he was gearing up for war. According to Strollo, Zottola went to talk to Genovese on Strollo's behalf, and what he allegedly brought back from the don was music to Strollo's ears: "Get rid of them. Get them out of town." Strollo went to Altshuler to take care of Biondillo once and for all. Altshuler gave Strollo his word that Biondillo would be killed, and the planning started.[257]

Bob Kroner, the lead FBI agent in Youngstown for organized crime and the man who had been targeting the crew there for years, was considered by Strollo to be his main law enforcement nemesis. Kroner got a tip from an informant that Strollo was going to kill Biondillo. According to the *New Republic*, Kroner was obligated to warn Biondillo of the threat based on FBI protocol. Kroner asked Biondillo if he knew who he was on the phone, and Biondillo responded in the affirmative. They met later that night in a parking lot. Kroner was hoping Biondillo would become a cooperator in the case. Instead, he just kept saying, "Who the fuck wants to kill me?" Kroner could not tell him, as it would have led to immediate violence, but given Biondillo's long feud with Strollo, he would have to have been an idiot not to figure it out.[258] Biondillo wasn't stupid and started to wear a bullet-proof vest some of the time while he traveled around town.

Altshuler and Riddle's hit team consisted of Lavance Turnage, Warren Willis, Cleveland Blair and George Wilkins. Altshuler and Riddle had been using some of their drug dealing associates to watch Biondillo to get his routines down. Riddle, Turnage and Wilkins drove around with guns in their car to kill Biondillo but could not find him. After this, Riddle decided to delegate responsibilities for the actual hit and recruited some more people to replace him on the team. After the first failed attempt, they thought they had found the perfect stretch of road to ambush the mobster. The route was one Biondillo used on his way to work at Youngstown United Music. Murdock Street in Youngstown was a desolate and deserted place. The street was one-way and extremely narrow for a quarter mile; only one car could fit through. The road was lined with derelict vehicles in neglected yards, run-down homes and trash. It was the ideal place to kill someone and get away with it.

On the morning of June 3, 1996, the temperature was about sixty degrees Fahrenheit with a light wind blowing. Ernie Biondillo was driving his Cadillac down the little deserted cut-through to his headquarters at Center Street and Wilson Avenue. Biondillo was confronted with a car blocking his way, its hood up as if in distress. Lavance Turnage was the driver. Biondillo started to back down Murdock Street to take another way into town. Warren Willis pulled up behind him in another car to block him from leaving the scene. Cleveland Blair and George Wilkins were waiting for Biondillo, hiding behind a nearby house with shotguns at the ready. When they saw the gangster become trapped by their fellow hit team members, they pulled their ski masks down, ran over to Biondillo's car and unloaded into him. The shotgun blasts broke through the rolled-up windows and decimated

Left: Naples's and Biondillo's former Youngstown United Music in 2022. *Courtesy of an anonymous researcher.*

Right: Biondillo as an older man (*far right, with cigar*). *Courtesy of an anonymous researcher.*

Biondillo's head.[259] One of the team members reached into the car and grabbed Biondillo's signature gold and diamond ring that had his initials "EB" from his dead hand.[260] Afterward, the four men went for lunch and received their piece of the $35,000 contract murder fee.

The hit was big news in Youngstown. Strollo did not kill Biondillo in a low-key way. The body and car were left in the street as a warning to the Center Street crew. Their time was over, and Strollo was confirmed as the Pittsburgh family's man in charge of Youngstown. The hit was the beginning of a new era for Strollo, a time when he would start throwing caution to the wind and use extreme measures to get what he wanted. He had not always been this way, but something had changed in the old man.

DECLARING WAR ON THE LAW

A few months before the Biondillo killing, Strollo, Altshuler and Riddle started to utilize the services of Mark Batcho. The "Nut," as Strollo had called him, was not only feared by Strollo's side in the brewing mafia civil war, but he was also seen as someone who could become a useful enforcer for Strollo's crew. Employing him was also a clever way to neutralize Batcho without actually having to kill him. In March 1996, Batcho assassinated sixty-six-year-old Boardman, Ohio businessman Lawrence Sisman, who was a close associate of Ernie Biondillo's old crew. Sisman was Biondillo's partner in the Palace in the Pines Bar and Strip Club. According to an interview with Batcho, he killed Sisman once he realized the Center Street crew did not like him due to his alleged bad business decisions.[261] Batcho had also been fired by Sisman from his job at the Palace at the Pines after he knocked a cop out who was causing trouble in the bar. The unapproved hit on Sisman almost got Batcho killed, but Biondillo protected him from the other Center Street crew associates. Batcho wanted to be made into the mob more than anything, and to him, Biondillo was a personal hero. He even had a tattoo of Biondillo on his body.

Gary Van Brocklin, a former Mahoning County prosecutor and current defense attorney in March 1996, was defending Lavance Turnage in an assault case that had proven difficult to fix due to the judge not being on Strollo's payroll. Turnage was facing multiple years in prison to the chagrin of Bernie Altshuler. Altshuler wanted to fix the case by utilizing corrupted Mahoning County prosecutor Jimmy Philomena. However, they needed a postponement, and Van Brocklin was saying that was not possible. In response, Strollo's group was determined to have Van Brocklin replaced by their main fixer and lawyer Mike Rich. George Alexander, the disbarred lawyer who managed bribe payments to Philomena, suggested that Strollo wound Van Brocklin to get the postponement. On Monday, April Fool's Day 1996, Batcho and Riddle parked near Van Brocklin's law office across the street from the county courthouse in the heart of downtown Youngstown in a stolen car. Riddle acted as a spotter and waited near the front door while Batcho entered the law office with a walkie-talkie and a silenced handgun. Batcho asked the man he saw as he walked into the office if his name was Attorney Gary Van Brocklin. Van Brocklin answered, "Yes, I am." And Batcho immediately shot him in the knee.[262]

In the same month, James Philomena lost the Democratic primary for the Mahoning County prosecutor's office to Paul Gains. Paul Gains was driven and had the experience of being a steelworker, Youngstown cop and defense attorney behind him. He promised to help clean up his town and was assured the prosecutor's spot after the primary, since no candidates were running against him in the general election. Strollo thought he had two people who would have inroads into corrupting Gains, but those avenues failed. George Alexander, according to Strollo, wanted Altshuler and Riddle

Prosecutor Paul Gains. *Courtesy of the Mahoning County Prosecutor's Office.*

to kill the prosecutor so that Philomena could fill in until a new prosecutor could be chosen. Strollo was further motivated to take this plan of action when he heard rumors on the street that Gains would hire FBI agent Bob Kroner, Strollo's old nemesis, to be a county investigator. Strollo decided to eliminate Gains and went to Altshuler and Riddle to handle it. They included Mo Man Harris and Batcho on the hit team.

Strollo was now marching into uncharted territory for the Pittsburgh mafia, and even though other mafia families had contemplated and even tried similar attacks on prosecutors, they always ended badly for those involved.[263]

Declaring war on the county government was a foolish and far too aggressive move for Strollo to keep his corrupted officials in power. Unlike the Biondillo hit, there is no mention of Mike Genovese approving of the plan to kill Gains. Genovese's normal mode of operation points to the fact that he would have been horrified of a move against a prosecutor. It seemed Strollo was going out on a limb, possibly due to his overseer Zottola having problems with his health and the government from 1996 onward emboldening Strollo, given his apparent independence.[264]

If the hit succeeded, Strollo wanted to have his personal pet Mike Rich as the next county prosecutor. Business would be exceptionally good for fixing cases if he could get him in office. In October 1996, Riddle, Turnage and Wilkins tried to kill Gains at a Youngstown restaurant. The armed hit team sat at their table and watched Gains eat with his colleagues. The attempt was abandoned after they noticed a heavy police presence in the area and the restaurant filled up with rowdy college kids. Riddle replaced Turnage on the hit team since he had to plead guilty to an earlier robbery charge and went to prison.

THE HIT

Paul Gains was planning for a fun time out at the tail end of 1996. It had been a good year, and soon, he would be the new Mahoning County prosecutor. On the cold and rainy night of December 23, he left his office at around 8:00 p.m. and went to a local bar with some friends. He left that bar and then hung out at the Caffe Capri in Boardman, Ohio. He stayed there until 1:00 a.m. and then started for home.

According to the *New Republic* and the *Cleveland Scene*, at the same time Gains was having a few drinks, Strollo's hit team was planning to kill Gains at his residence. Riddle, Batcho and Harris had assembled walkie-talkies, ski masks, gloves, a police scanner and a revolver to welcome Gains home mafia style. The team came to the house and found it empty. Batcho exited the vehicle and waited by the garage. He had a speed loader with him for the revolver and a walkie-talkie. He tested the radio, but no one answered, so he went back to the car. The three men traveled to a Giant Eagle grocery store parking lot and enabled a one-touch dial feature on two cellphones for quick communication in lieu of the radio.

As they returned to the house, they saw Gains's car was in the driveway and the lights were on. Riddle gave Batcho the gun again, and Batcho exited the car. Batcho was carrying a bag of cocaine with him so that it could be planted on Gains's body. They hoped it would make the hit look like a drug-related killing. Batcho was nervous as he approached the house. He had killed and hurt people before, but this was a government official—it was different. The garage door and side door were wide open since Gains had let his cats out just moments before. Gains was on the phone as Batcho walked into his kitchen. Batcho raised the pistol and fired. Gains fell to the ground, and Batcho fired a second time, missing Gains and hitting his caller ID box. Gains was badly wounded in his forearm and side by the first bullet. Batcho stepped up, aimed at the prosecutor's heart—and the gun jammed.

Batcho panicked and ran out of the house, running into some woods out back and falling as he ran. He got back up and used the one-touch feature on his cellphone to call his accomplices. Batcho yelled into the phone that he had done the deed and needed to be picked up. Batcho jumped into the backseat, and Riddle asked him if Gains was dead. Batcho answered uncertainly and then blurted out that the gun had jammed. Riddle was about to have the team go back into the house to finish the job, but the police scanner alerted them to the fact that the cops were on their way. Riddle sped away from the scene while Harris threw the gun out the window. In the meantime, Gains had tried to use his home phone to call for help, but Batcho's shot to the caller ID box had knocked the phone out. Gains reached for his cellphone and called 911. Gains then passed out while thinking about how his mother would handle the news of his murder.

Batcho had lost his speed loader at the scene. However, there was not much in the way of evidence. Gains had gotten only a fleeting look at his attacker. The speed loader yielded no clues, and all the police found was one clear footprint. It seemed the hit team would get away with their crime. Gains was sworn in as county prosecutor ten days later. The mafia had failed to stop him from taking office. Due to the bungling attempt to kill Gains, he and the police did not believe it was the mob that wanted him dead. They did not know who it was, but the Cosa Nostra was not at the top of the list. Gains believed that if the mafia had wanted to kill him, they would have succeeded.[265]

THE BEGINNING OF THE END

In the winter of 1995, a Strollo-controlled illegal gambling Super Bowl party was raided by the FBI, and Garono and Dante were arrested. The mafia knew the FBI was always watching, but they did not know that this time, the agents were determined to take Strollo and his entire enterprise down. The investigation would last for years, and the Super Bowl raid started a chain reaction that would eventually turn into gold for the Department of Justice.

The 1995 Super Bowl arrests and raid led to a gambler and bookie named Michael Sabella cooperating and wearing a wire against mob-affiliated bookie Michael Serrecchio. The Serrecchio conversations and others allowed agents to get enough evidence to bug various mob-affiliated locations and gambling spots. This second round of wiretaps caught Strollo and Garono talking about bribing the Mahoning County sheriff Phil Chance. The evidence eventually allowed the FBI to bug Strollo's big farmhouse in Canfield, Ohio, through his phone and a microphone in his kitchen. Strollo suspected his phone was tapped but continued to talk about bribing officials and other mafia business. To his credit, he did try to mask the conversations by speaking in code. The fact of the matter is that the gangsters in the Mahoning Valley were so used to running everything that they allowed themselves to be less than careful, even when they knew they were under scrutiny. The feds eventually turned Garono, Strollo's brother Dante and many others.

The trial against Strollo and his associates became a little frightening for the cooperating witnesses when one of them received a dead finch in a manila envelope that had been mailed from Pittsburgh to their office.[266]

In addition, a bullet was fired and hit one of the prison windows where Batcho, the former hit man and soon to be cooperating witness, was staying. The police stated the bullet was likely a stray and not related to mafia intimidation.[267]

THE ULTIMATE BETRAYAL

At this point, Strollo, Altshuler, Riddle and Turnage were alone in staying true to the vow of silence in organized crime. Worse was to come. A scorned girlfriend of one of the associates of the hit team members who had tried to kill Gains, George Wilkins of the Biondillo murder squad, called Gains up directly and told him she knew who had tried to kill him.[268] According to Gains, the woman called him about the crimes of her boyfriend and his associates since he had borrowed her car and it had been torched by one of Wilkins's enemies. The torched car was parked in front of the house of a woman whom Wilkins was allegedly cheating on his girlfriend with.

Gains called law enforcement, and soon, Batcho, Riddle, Harris and Altshuler were arrested for their parts in the assassination plot.[269] It was a lucky break from a scorned woman that could be right out of a Hollywood movie script. Harris and Batcho turned on their former allies. Wilkins, one of the Biondillo assassins who had stolen the dead mobster's "EB" ring, was also called out in court when law enforcement was able to connect him to the one-of-a-kind jewelry based on testimony from the Pittsburgh pawn shop owner he sold it to.

In December 1997, the FBI arrested twenty-eight mafia associates and Lenny Strollo. In February 1999, after realizing he would spend the rest of his life in jail, Strollo also betrayed his friends and testified against Altshuler, Riddle and Turnage. Two Black men and a Jewish man who could never be made took omerta more seriously than an actual member of Cosa Nostra. Strollo did not only deliver his loyal underlings to the Department of Justice, but he also gave information and testimony against the public officials he had used to control the Mahoning Valley for the benefit of himself and the Pittsburgh mob since at least 1991. Altshuler, Riddle and Turnage were convicted of the murders and other crimes outlined previously and sentenced to life in prison. Riddle, the Black man who dreamed of being inducted into the mob, gave a smirk and a defiant burp in court after the jury handed down the guilty verdict. The curtain call of the Youngstown crew ended not with a bang but with a belch.

By the mid-2000s, Strollo's testimony and the FBI's hard work had led to over seventy convictions of public officials, mobsters and others. The government had to make a deal with Strollo, the Pittsburgh family's lead representative in Youngstown and a confessed lifetime criminal and murderer, but the Mahoning Valley could finally start to heal from the mafia abscess that had hooked itself onto the region for so many decades. Strollo was released from prison in 2012 and lived out his remaining days in the Mahoning Valley until he died at the ripe old age of ninety in 2021.[270]

8

ECHOES OF A DYING BORGATA

Maybe I can ease some of the pain I've caused.[271]

—*Charles "Chucky" Porter*

The Last Decade Begins

As the year 2000 dawned, the Pittsburgh mafia limped into the new century. The 1990s, especially the year 1990, had been disastrous for the Borgata, with the destruction of the family's drug enterprise and middle management, the imprisonment of multiple members and associates and the annihilation of the Wheeling and Youngstown crews. The family was on the verge of extinction due to the advanced age of its members, effective prosecutions of key figures and the devastating transformation of Lenine Strollo into a government witness.

Cleansing the Unions

The 1990s and the early 2000s also saw the exposure of one of the mafia's longtime power bases: the labor unions. The Pittsburgh mob's foray into the unions is not very well documented, and it does not appear that the family was able to use the local unions to completely control construction, garbage hauling and other industries like the five families in New York. Pittsburgh's union ties were there but rarely resulted in headlines. In 1969, LaRocca was indicted federally in a rare attempt to hold the cagey mob boss to account for his crimes. Four other Pittsburgh mob members were charged along with him for using a kickback scheme to increase a loan from the pension fund for the International Brotherhood of Teamsters in Chicago. The case never went anywhere, but the incident illustrated Pittsburgh's place in the mob's control of unions and the attempts to use that control for profit. The teamster's fraud LaRocca was indicted on also involved Cosa Nostra players in Detroit and New York.[272]

Local 211 of the Teamsters represented Pittsburgh's newspaper delivery drivers. The longtime head of the local was a man named Theodore Cozza. Cozza was also a vice-president on the international's general executive board. In the late 1980s, the Justice Department sued the Teamsters under the RICO statute's civil code to accept the oversight of a federal administrator. The union was also forced to provide office space for an in-house investigation team that would root out corruption and organized crime ties in the union. It was against the union's own rules to bring reproach upon the union, and the oversight personnel interpreted the reproach clause as covering association with organized crime figures.

The investigations of organized crime association were meant to eject any union officers who violated the reproach rule. The oversight team also retooled the union's elections to make them more secretive and direct, so no one could be intimidated to vote one way or another. The elections in Pittsburgh were likely to turn out with Cozza's victory despite any changes in the union's election policies, since he seemed to be genuinely popular. A deluge of support from rank-and-file union employees was expressed during the proceedings against Cozza.[273]

Cozza was reportedly a highly effective union president who obtained some of the highest wages in the business for the drivers he represented. He was also feared by newspaper executives and would not hesitate to use work stoppages to negotiate. In 1992, after Cozza left the *Pittsburgh Press*, a final work stoppage helped create the conditions that ended the newspaper's run forever. The *Pittsburgh Press* was sold to the *Pittsburgh Post-Gazette* that year.

Cozza's ties to organized crime were undeniable and were hurting the reputation of Local 211. At a hearing in July 1990, the government outlined that Cozza had regularly met with John LaRocca at Allegheny Car Wash. Some of the meetings between the two had been recorded on video or in photographs. Cozza was also taped meeting with Mike Genovese, Kelly Mannarino, Jo Jo Pecora, Antonio Ripepi and Joseph Sica. Cozza also attended the funeral of Pittsburgh made member Louis Volpe and even kissed Mike Genovese when greeting him one time. Cozza denied ever discussing Teamsters' business with the mobsters.[274] Cozza was acquitted of charges related to bribery in exchange for labor peace in 1960, and Cozza invoked the Fifth Amendment thirty-five times during his testimony to the United States Senate Rackets Committee.[275] However, no charges or allegations were ever proven against Cozza or Local 211.

The proceedings in the early 1990s were merely about whether Cozza associated with members of organized crime and whether that was enough to oust him from the union. In January 1991, Cozza was ousted from his beloved union for his organized crime ties after forty-one years of leading Local 211. He died in 1996.

In March 2000, almost ten years after the Local 211 proceedings, the Department of Justice used a consent decree to get rid of alleged corruption and mob infiltration at Local 1058 of the Laborers International Union of North America. The government and the union's parent organization itself alleged that Joseph LaQuatra, the business manager of the local since 1985, had a leading role in the corrupt practices of the union. LaQuatra was a champion Golden Gloves boxer, a local businessman and an inductee into the National Italian American Sports Hall of Fame. The complaint alleged that seven leading union members had close "personal, family and business connections" to organized crime figures in the Pittsburgh family. It was alleged that the union members in question had participated in hiring ghost employees, loansharking, illegal gambling and associating with known mob figures. Others targeted in the probe were union president L. Dennis Martire, Gerald Pecora Jr., Philip Ameris, Mark Machi, Joseph Frydrych and John LaRocca Jr. Pecora Jr. was the great nephew of deceased Pittsburgh underboss Jo Jo Pecora, and LaRocca Jr. was the son of mob boss John LaRocca Sr. Ameris was the son of an alleged mob associate.

The head of the local before LaQuatra, Thomas Pecora, had been charged in 1971 with diverting union funds to buy a piece of property off John LaRocca Sr. at an inflated overmarket price. The complaint also stated that the old don had handpicked LaQuatra to be Pecora's successor. The allegations also stated the elections in the union had gone uncontested for thirty years. LaQuatra, Martire and Pecora Jr. were also alleged to have met with LaRocca at Allegheny Car Wash like Cozza of Local 211 had.[276]

According to the *Pittsburgh Post-Gazette*, in March 2001, the union was ordered to accept oversight from an appointed supervisor who monitored the local's deals with contractors and membership meetings. The supervisor also had the power to override decisions made by the union's officers and remove the officers if needed. LaQuatra resigned from his position in the union the year before when the allegations were made public, and he died in 2010.[277] No actual crimes were ever prosecuted or charged related to the 2000–1 probe of Local 1058.[278]

SONNY'S GAME AND THE LAST GAMBLERS

Thomas "Sonny" Ciancutti was the made member in charge of what was left of the New Kensington and Westmoreland County rackets after former underboss Kelly Mannarino died in 1980. In June 1960, Ciancutti was running a casino in New Kensington with mob associate Abe Zeid that had barbut and dice games on the first floor and horse betting on the second floor in the Garibaldi building. The joint was raided by authorities, with Ciancutti mugging for cameras while his associates scrambled to hide their faces. Ciancutti was found guilty of charges related to illegal gambling by a federal jury.[279] Ciancutti was fined $25,000 and given two years' probation. It was not enough to stop the young crime figure from staying in the business and thriving for the next four decades. Marvin Droznek, the mob associate and government witness, testified that his mentor, made member Frank Amato Jr., had to pay Ciancutti $20,000 at a meeting in the mid-1980s to stay out of his territory in Braddock. Droznek brought a gun to the meeting but luckily did not need to use it.[280]

Ciancutti was the cousin of drug dealer Gary Golden. According to one of the Pittsburgh mob's drug suppliers and a Florida-based former undercover FBI agent named Daniel Mitrione, Ciancutti was on the scene when Golden tested cocaine samples before particularly big deals.[281] Mitrione turned against the FBI and became corrupted by the Florida drug suppliers, becoming what he was supposed to be fighting against, an associate of organized crime.

Thomas "Sonny" Ciancutti.
Courtesy of the Pennsylvania State Archives.

According to a former FBI agent, a news article and a book, Ciancutti was also allegedly involved in skimming profits from a Seminole bingo operation on a reservation in Florida. The skim had been set up through the bingo hall's management company, much like the organization that managed the Rincon Casino, although this scheme reportedly lasted much longer, possibly into the 1990s. Mannarino and Meyer Lansky had set the deal up in the late 1970s, just before their deaths. Ciancutti would reportedly go down to Florida quite often to pick up Pittsburgh's piece of the action and drive it back north after playing high-stakes gin at Turnberry Isle during the winter months.[282]

MR. BROWN IS BUSTED

In October 2000, State of Pennsylvania authorities arrested seventy-year-old Sonny Ciancutti for running a sports betting operation in Allegheny and Fayette Counties with ten other people. Ciancutti allegedly received a 10 percent tribute from the ring. The ring brought in $500,000 a week during football season and $300,000 a week during basketball season. The head of the Fayette County side of the operation that covered sports betting and numbers gambling was Jeffrey Risha, while the Allegheny County side had sports betting and video poker machines under Ralph Maselli. Both men reported to Ciancutti, who was referred to in code as "Mr. Brown." Ciancutti accepted tribute from his lieutenants and lower-level bookies and loansharks. The ring also continued to use the threat of violence to collect on lost bets from reluctant customers.[283]

The investigation against Ciancutti's gamblers was complex and involved surveillance and wiretaps and forced coconspirators to testify before a state grand jury through grants of immunity. Ciancutti listed himself as an executive in Wright Industries Incorporated in Greentree, but a manager at the company told the grand jury he was never an employee and that the manager had been ordered to add Ciancutti to the company rolls by the company's president in 1996. This incident shows the pull that Ciancutti's name still had as late as the mid-1990s.[284]

Ciancutti pleaded no contest to one felony racketeering charge and was sentenced to ninety days of house arrest and twenty months of probation in March 2002. Ciancutti had gotten off with a slap on the wrist again.[285] Ciancutti would die a free man many years later in July 2021 of natural causes. He was the last made man in the Pittsburgh mafia at that time. The last remnant of the family was gone.

However, old mob associates continued to make the news after Ciancutti's 2002 sentencing. Jon Scalzitti, one of Louis Raucci's alleged drug dealers, was prosecuted again in 2004, after he and an associate teamed up with a member of the Pagans motorcycle gang to distribute an estimated $11 million in marijuana, cocaine and methamphetamine in western Pennsylvania.[286] Ninety-year-old Robert Iannelli and his son, who took over a piece of the aforementioned Tony Grosso's gambling empire in the 1980s, when Grosso went to prison, pleaded guilty to running an illegal lottery and sports betting operation in Westmoreland and Allegheny Counties in September 2020. Iannelli once paid a portion of his profits to the Pittsburgh mob. He was sentenced to pay hefty fines and serve probation for his crimes after a state investigation ended the illegal gambling enterprise in 2017.[287] There were many other gambling prosecutions throughout the 2000s and 2010s that caught former Pittsburgh mob associates doing what they had always done: taking people's bets.

FINAL BETRAYAL

In November 2000, the aging remains of the Pittsburgh mafia received a terrible shock. The imprisoned Charles Porter, one of the most talented and trusted mafia leaders in Pittsburgh's modern Cosa Nostra, was an informant. Porter was once second in command of the family from 1987 to 1990, and now, he had betrayed the oath he took in front of Mike Genovese to keep the mob's secrets under pain of death. Porter had been an undercover informant for years while imprisoned and used his contacts with other mob inmates and with his old family while incarcerated to report some particularly useful information to the FBI.

At first, Porter had rebuffed efforts by the FBI to get him to cooperate after he was sentenced to twenty-eight years in prison. Then, according to Porter, his health began failing, and he started to think about seeing his family again. Porter was diabetic, and it was affecting his kidneys and eyesight.

Porter's cooperation with the FBI began in 1992, a little over a year after his landmark Pittsburgh trial. FBI agents Roger Greenbank and Robert Garrity testified that Porter's assistance was key to stopping mob murders and moving other prosecutions forward. They argued that he should be released from prison. At the time of their testimony, Porter had served ten and a half years of his twenty-eight-year-long sentence. The details Porter learned from other mafia members and associates about future mob hits helped the FBI stop those planned murders, relocate witnesses and fix vulnerabilities in the witness protection program that allowed people like Porter to get information about protected informants.

Porter even gave investigators information about a planned hit on former Pittsburgh mob associate and government witness Joey Rosa, who had testified against Porter at his trial. The family hierarchy found out about Rosa's plans to travel back to Pittsburgh to visit family, and a hit was sanctioned to take Rosa out. Rosa and his family were warned because of Porter, and Rosa lived to tell the tale. Porter also saved the life of former Philadelphia underboss and government witness Phil Leonetti, who had been marked for death by the Philadelphia family. In total, Porter saved the lives of six people targeted by the mob for assassination.

In 1993, Porter informed the FBI of a plot to kill an ex–mob boss who had become an informant. In 1995, he told them that a Boston mob member was going to kill an individual when he got out of prison. Also in 1995, Porter learned of a plot by a Pittsburgh mobster to murder a suspected informant. Porter also gave valuable information to the FBI about the Pittsburgh family's scheme to take over the Rincon Casino and revealed intelligence about the family's operations in Youngstown.[288]

Porter's son, lawyer Charles Porter Jr., represented him at the court proceeding in an emotional display of fealty from father to son. Porter Jr.'s arguments, combined with the testimony of the FBI agents, were powerful testaments to Porter Sr.'s cooperation.

Porter's cooperation paid off. He was released in 2000 and lived with his family in the same house he had lived in when he was the underboss of the Pittsburgh family. No one made a known attempt on his life, and his old colleagues seemingly left him alone.

Porter never testified against Genovese. Porter had perjured himself at his trial numerous times while he testified in his own defense, and this fact precluded using Porter against his old boss in court.[289] In the end, the FBI considered building a tax violation case against Genovese, but the evidence was just not that strong without Porter's testimony. Porter's defense strategy of lying on the stand did a lousy job of helping Porter, but it seems to have helped Genovese stay out of prison.[290]

Assessment

In the late 1980s, according to an interviewed source who wishes to remain anonymous, Genovese met with Vincent Gigante of New York's Genovese family to ask to induct even more new members for Pittsburgh. Gigante allegedly told him to hold off until the family's prosecution troubles passed.

John Bazzano Jr. was allegedly Genovese's last underboss. *Courtesy of the Pennsylvania State Archives.*

In addition, the rule remained in effect that new members could be inducted only if an old member died. Genovese did not make any new members after the group of four or five he had initiated earlier in the 1980s. In this author's opinion, the defections of Rosa, Strollo and Porter convinced him to allow the family to die of old age. Genovese may have also thought of his promise to himself back in 1974, when he reportedly swore he would never go back to prison.

Genovese's crime family, despite its troubles in the 1980s and 1990s, had more than a few members die in bed at home rather than in prison like so many higher-ranking mafia figures in other cities. The Cleveland mob's soldiers and hierarchy languished in prison for most of the period this book covers, while Genovese, Imburgia, Bazzano Jr., Amato Jr., Ciancutti, Capizzi and Ferruccio lived seemingly quiet lives at home with periodic interruptions of attempted prosecution that usually resulted in fines, probation or a short jail term for gambling or other white-collar crimes. The only members in the 1980s and 1990s who faced serious repercussions from death, prison or both were Porter, Raucci, Zottola, Strollo, Naples, Verilla and, to a lesser extent, Pecora.

If seen in this light, the Pittsburgh mob was a criminal success for a good chunk of its membership at this time. It was and still is unheard of for a family boss to stay out of prosecutor's hands for as long as Mike Genovese did. The FBI had a squad dedicated to his destruction, with talented agents from Pittsburgh and Cleveland gunning for his Borgata. His decision to look the other way as his family became involved in the drug trade was a mistake that made the good guys' jobs easier, but he was smart and careful enough not to make it a fatal one for his freedom. Genovese and Porter's unlikely partnership had brought the mob in Pittsburgh to the pinnacle of criminal power and profit and then, after a few years, cast it down to the edge of extinction.

According to an interview conducted by the *Pittsburgh Post-Gazette*, as Roger Greenbank left his job at the FBI in Pittsburgh, he drove by Genovese's big brown house off Clendenning Road in West Deer one last time in the summer of 1999. He saw the old man engaging in one of his favorite pastimes, enjoying his property and riding his tractor in his garden

Mike Genovese smoking a cigar on his tractor. *Courtesy of an anonymous researcher.*

Part of the team that brought the mob low: the FBI's Roger Greenbank (*left*), federal prosecutor Bruce Teitelbaum (*right*) and IRS agent Ed Reiser (*center*). *Courtesy of the* Pittsburgh Post-Gazette.

Michael James Genovese, the last real "godfather of Pittsburgh." *Courtesy of the Pennsylvania State Archives.*

with his shirt off on a sunny day. Greenbank drove by, and Genovese waved. Greenbank waved back, and that was it.[291] Genovese died of congestive heart disease and bladder cancer in his sleep at home under the care of his third wife on Halloween, October 31, 2006. He was eighty-seven years old. Roger Greenbank told the *Pittsburgh Post-Gazette*, "He beat us at the game."[292]

There was barely anything left of the Pittsburgh mob after Genovese's passing. After a few years, at least some of what remained of the gambling associates worked for themselves or paid a percentage to some of the old made guys who still lived. The odd gambling bust every few years is evidence that the old associates are still hustling out there.

The Pittsburgh mob had a tumultuous run of at least nine decades under seven bosses. Not one of them died in prison. Three were killed by assassins, and four died of natural causes at home. The Pittsburgh mob was a criminal success for a long time. However, many people were beaten, killed, robbed, assaulted, wronged by corrupt officials and turned into addicts, thieves, prostitutes and debtors all so the men who ran the Pittsburgh mob could live lives of leisure, wealth and adventure. The mob makes for a remarkable story, and the tough guys who inhabited that world definitely had their rockstar moments, but let us never forget the piles of victims crushed under the weight of their criminal successes. Law enforcement was right to destroy the Borgata as much as they did, and the fight continues against other organized crime groups and gangs that have taken their place.

9

UNSOLVED

The following few cases represent some of the more infamous unsolved incidents that are allegedly connected to the mafia in Pittsburgh. No one was ever convicted of these crimes. According to media reports, court testimony, FBI information and Pennsylvania State Police information, Pittsburgh mob associates and members were allegedly involved in each of these three instances.

"WE DO MILLION-DOLLAR SCORES"

On St. Patrick's Day, March 17, 1982, at 11:30 p.m., fifty-four-year-old Purolator armored car service security guard James Powers was inside his company's terminal in an alley off Brownsville Road in Pittsburgh, guarding over $55 million in cash. He had just watched one of the armored trucks leave the secure garage for a delivery to Pittsburgh International Airport. He had the vault open to get ready for the next delivery of $2.5 million, which had been separated from the rest of the money in the facility. As the delivery truck left and the garage door started to close again, two men dressed in trench coats, with hats and sunglasses on, slipped underneath the door and approached Powers while holding up what appeared to be FBI credentials and carrying walkie-talkies. Powers let his guard down when the men identified themselves as FBI agents and stated they were at the facility to warn Powers that they had a tip the place would be robbed.

They got very close to Powers and quickly grabbed the shotgun right out of his hands. They then turned him around and grabbed the pistol from his holster, handcuffed him, tied his legs around the ankles and taped his eyes shut. The duo then hit Powers over the head and placed him face-down on the concrete floor. Powers then heard the robbers on their walkie-talkies, speaking to a third person, likely the getaway driver. A brief time later, a vehicle pulled into the garage, and the men wheeled over the $2.5 million shipment in steel carts loaded with thirty bags of $5, $10, $20, $50 and $100 bills. The men left with their loot, leaving the remaining $55 million in the vault, and Powers was able to struggle for ninety minutes to get to a phone to call a stranger's number. His hands were still bound, and he could not dial correctly. He eventually managed to convince the individual to call 911 to report the crime. It was the greatest heist in western Pennsylvania history, and the three men who pulled it off have never been held to account for their spectacular crime. This was due to a lack of physical evidence left at the scene, the men's disguises and there being only one credible witness.[293]

The only break in the case came during the Porter trial in 1990. Joey Rosa, the former mob associate and government witness, testified that Geno Chiarelli, also a mob associate, had bragged about committing the robbery while in Florida with Rosa in April 1985 to consummate a drug deal. Chiarelli allegedly said of Rosa's associate: "What are you doing with this idiot? He is a nickel-dime guy. We do million-dollar scores." Rosa then said on the stand that Chiarelli informed him of how the heist went, including

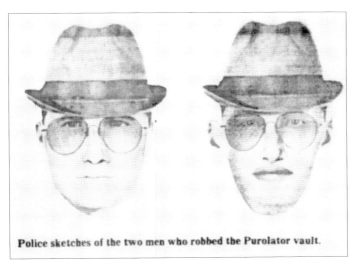

Police sketches of the two men who robbed the Purolator vault.

Police sketch of the Purolator suspects. *As reprinted in the* Pittsburgh Post-Gazette.

The Purolator terminal. *Courtesy of the* Pittsburgh Post-Gazette.

that Chiarelli had dressed up as an FBI agent. According to an interview with Porter conducted by a former FBI agent, a piece of the Purolator job's action went from Chiarelli to Porter and then on to Genovese.[294]

Chiarelli was a colorful mob character and was convicted of the 1986 theft of $2 million worth of antique rifles from First Seneca Bank in Greensburg, Pennsylvania, after he and a team of thieves cut a hole in the roof, disconnected an alarm and drilled a hole in the vault. He and an accomplice had fled from federal agents who were trying to arrest them in Florida and almost hit a school bus during an eighty-mile-per-hour chase. Chiarelli got away during the chaos but turned himself in to federal authorities in Pittsburgh a brief time later.[295] He was also convicted of drug-related offenses during the Porter trial and was in prison until 2008.[296] Rosa's information about the Purolator robbery went nowhere prosecution-wise, and the five-year statute of limitations on the crime had already expired anyway. Whoever did the crime, it was the opinion of law enforcement officials that the perpetrators were connected to organized crime due to the professionalism of the job.[297]

"Keep Your Mouth Shut
and Don't Make Any More Waves"

On October 24, 1988, around 6:30 p.m., thirty-two-year-old Robert Mancini walked back to his first-floor apartment on Third Street in McKee's Rocks, Pennsylvania, where he lived with a relative. McKee's Rocks was a tough gambling town situated next to the Ohio River and full of working-class folks descended from European immigrants who thought nothing of numbers, sports betting, video poker and card games. It was harmless fun to them and as normal as going to church every week. The games themselves may have just been a way to pass the time and possibly win some extra spending money, but the men who ran those games were deadly serious. Mancini was one of those men, and he had a lot on his mind as he walked home.[298]

Mancini was a bookie, a ward committeeman in the Democratic Party, and the manager of his family's restaurant named Mancini's Lounge. He was also facing state gambling charges after getting busted twice in the last few years for running illegal card games out of the lounge. The arrests did not stop Mancini, and he continued to run a numbers operation using the Pennsylvania Lottery's drawings. Mancini also had video poker machines at a place he owned called Robert's Snack Shop and took sports bets. Police estimated Mancini's numbers operation dealt with about $2,000 worth of business a day. To keep his illegal business safe, Mancini allegedly paid McKees Rocks' mayor Dennis Skosnik, who was also a sheriff's deputy, $1,800 a month for protection. Mancini also gave money to charity and sponsored kids' baseball and football teams in the local area.[299]

The Rocks were usually a relatively quiet place back then—except for some brawling. It was not the type of town that came to mind when someone talked about murder. In the years before 1988, that changed somewhat. In January 1979, Jimmy Goodnight, a McKees Rocks street commissioner and ex-con, had just finished plowing the streets of snow when he took a swig from his customary bottle of whiskey to cut through the chill. He then went to visit with his friends in the police department, collapsed and later died. An investigation revealed that the whiskey he had consumed contained enough cyanide to kill seventy people. There were rumors in media and law enforcement circles about Goodnight being a mob loanshark in the Bottoms section of McKees Rocks, a bagman transporting payoffs to corrupt politicians or a gambler who could not pay his substantial debts. But nothing was ever confirmed, and the murderer was never caught and prosecuted.[300]

Robert Mancini
Betting a Rocks fact of life

Robert Mancini. *As printed in the*
Pittsburgh Post-Gazette.

In July 1987, Marty Fitzpatrick, a former McKees Rocks police officer, was near the Coffee Pot Restaurant in McKees Rocks after having visited a mob-run club and was robbed, beaten, strangled and then tied to the bumper of a car and dragged for a few blocks. Fitzpatrick had won some money while gambling, but a motive of robbery does not make sense given the way he was killed. Informants later told the state police that former mob underboss Kelly Mannarino hated Fitzpatrick for some unknown reason and left instructions that he should be murdered once he retired from the police force. Mannarino died in 1980, so if this story is true, his mob pals waited seven years to take his postmortem revenge.[301]

In 1988, Mancini was in a fight for his livelihood and his life. Adolph "Junior" Williams and his brother Eugene were expanding their alleged mafia-backed gambling operation into McKees Rocks in earnest. Several incidents of vandalism and intimidation had occurred—a firebombing here, a brick thrown through a window there—all to highlight that there were new players in town. Mancini even claimed that in the spring of 1988, a mobster drove Mancini to Allegheny Police Headquarters, where an official told him, "Junior Williams is the boss; keep your mouth shut and don't make any more waves." Williams then allegedly started to pay Mayor Skosnik more than Mancini could afford.[302]

The Williams brothers were the heirs to Tony Grosso's old gambling empire and were also planting the flag for Genovese's Borgata wherever they went. Mancini was incensed that these interlopers were invading what he saw as his turf and that they could steal his friend in the mayor's office so easily. Mancini reportedly had his own mafia mentor and backer named Anthony "Ninny the Torch" Lagatutta, a mob associate and convicted arsonist, but the Williams brothers were hard to stop. Soon, the Williamses took over a club that Mancini had his eye on, and Mancini had enough. He and Junior Williams got into a verbal altercation, and each allegedly vowed to eject the other from the Rocks.

Mancini did not have quite the amount of mob muscle that was available to Junior, but he did have one other option. His friend, the chief of the McKees Rocks police Ronald Panyko, offered to help Mancini if Mancini would

Adolph "Junior" Williams (*left*). *Courtesy of the* Pittsburgh Post-Gazette.

wear a wire. Mancini agreed to the request and assisted law enforcement in their attempt to bring down the corrupt politicians and gangsters in McKees Rocks as part of a wide-ranging state police investigation. The problem was that Mancini's cooperation with the state probe was leaked, and the mobsters soon found out.[303]

In the early evening of October 24, 1988, Mancini made it home and walked into his empty apartment. The relative who lived with him was out. He arrived sometime around 7:00 p.m. and quickly changed into more comfortable clothes. Mancini did not realize it, but he had been under surveillance by two McKees Rocks police officers who were told to break off about ten minutes before. According to one of the officers, Skosnik told them not to create a report for the surveillance that night.

Mancini turned the TV on to watch the lottery draw, laid out his betting slips for the day and called another bookie whom he laid bets off with. As he was talking on his red and white phone, someone must have knocked on his door. It appears he knew the person, as he apparently let them in and got back on his phone. He was sitting with the betting slips out in front of him on the dining room table, and the TV was showing static, as if he could not tune it correctly yet. A witness from across the street stated she saw a pickup truck pull up and a man get out and go into Mancini's apartment. At around 7:10 p.m., whoever the visitor was pulled out a .38 revolver, aimed it behind Mancini's

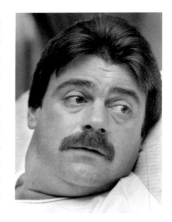

Dennis Skosnik. *Courtesy of the Pittsburgh Post-Gazette.*

right ear and pulled the trigger once. Mancini's head dropped on the table, and his hand was still gripping the phone receiver when he was found an hour later.[304]

His brother Anthony was enraged, and the next day, he allegedly went down to Hall's Café, saw Junior Williams sitting at a table at the bar and approached him. Williams reportedly extended his hand and started to convey his condolences when Anthony punched him and a short fight ensued. The fight was broken up.

No one ever paid the price for Mancini's murder. The case went cold, and the corruption charges against Mayor Skosnik melted away after the killing when key witnesses refused to testify against him. Skosnik eventually became chief deputy for the Allegheny County Sheriff's Office. In the mid-2000s, he was again prosecuted for corruption and went to prison for five years. Junior Williams was also prosecuted for gambling offenses during the same period and served four years.

Junior had a brief flirtation with fame when he was part of the 2014 A&E show *Godfather of Pittsburgh*, wherein a businessman and strip club owner from Pittsburgh, who was also Junior's son-in-law, acted as a wiseguy type of character. Junior lent the show a little legitimacy when he appeared as an advisor to his son-in-law, since Junior was a real gangster.[305] The true and last "godfather of Pittsburgh," the publicity-shy Mike Genovese, had to have been rolling in his grave. Junior died in 2016 of natural causes.[306]

THE DISAPPEARANCE OF JOSEPH BERTONE

Forty-nine-year-old Joseph Bertone was the owner of the popular Joey's Restaurant in McKeesport, but Bertone was no simple restaurateur. Bertone was a former boxer, an aspiring businessman and an alleged gangster. Bertone's restaurant was bombed in 1978 and then completely blown up in 1982. Both bombs were dynamite-based, with the 1982 explosion reportedly lifting the roof into the air and then collapsing it into the structure when it fell back down.[307] Bertone allegedly owed a lot of people money, and one suspect in the bombing was drug dealer John Heatherington.

In August 1982, Heatherington was shot in the head and face seven times in front of a hotel in North Versailles, Pennsylvania. Heatherington's death was reportedly ordered by Anthony LaRocca, the nephew of deceased Pittsburgh mob boss John LaRocca. Anthony was the leader of a local gang.[308] Bertone was an underworld player and tended to anger the wrong people in the business. He had a history of burglary, armed robbery, alleged loansharking and hijacking. The federal hijacking charge was thrown out in 1971, when the government's key witness was shot to death.[309]

Bertone was partners with Joey Rosa in Rosa and Porter's Florida drug deals until 1985. Bertone had gotten involved in the drug business due to crippling debt and desperately needing to get some quick cash to solve his financial problems that stemmed from the destruction of his restaurant.

Bertone and Rosa met in the summer of 1984 and became friends after a mutual acquaintance introduced them. Bertone advised Rosa on his scheme to rob his own jewelry store and provide the funds to the crime family's hierarchy. According to Rosa, this was the key payment that allowed Rosa to get into the good graces of Genovese and Porter. The duo then worked with Raucci and, later, Porter on drug deals through the mob's Colombian connection, Ramon Sosa, in Florida.

Joseph Bertone. *As printed in the* Pittsburgh Post-Gazette.

Rosa's testimony indicated that an April 1985 drug deal created friction between Bertone and Geno Chiarelli, who each blamed the other for being $6,000 short on a payment to Sosa for a shipment of drugs. The dispute became so heated that Porter had to be called in. Porter forced Bertone and Rosa to pay the missing money. Chiarelli was reportedly not a fan of Bertone after this incident.

Also, according to Rosa, Bertone and Chiarelli both knew the alleged father and son drug dealers George Jordan Sr. and George Jordan Jr. Bertone, still desperate for money in the spring of 1985, allegedly sold the Jordans a fake shipment of cocaine, which was actually sugar, for $100,000. Bertone then stole the shipment so that the Jordans would think a third party had taken the drugs. The convoluted scheme seemed to work, as Jordan Jr., according to Rosa, came to Bertone to borrow $100,000 at a high interest rate to replace the funds lost in the bad deal. Jordan Jr. denied Rosa's story in full and stated it was all a lie during the Porter trial.

The Jordans were in business with Bertone prior to all this alleged drama as co-owners of his restaurant, so they may have trusted him to be an honest partner. Chiarelli would allegedly make sure the Jordans never trusted Bertone again. In May 1985, Bertone told a relative that he had fought with Chiarelli after Chiarelli reportedly told the Jordans that Bertone had ripped them off of the $100,000.[310]

At 9:30 p.m. on June 17, 1985, Bertone left his McKeesport residence. As Bertone left, his wife asked him to bring home Pepsi and milk. Bertone called her from his car phone in his 1985 white Cadillac Seville at 10:00 p.m. and told her he would be at the Jordan's truck garage if anyone called the house. Rosa called Bertone a few minutes later, and Bertone answered his car phone after a few rings, as if he were outside of his vehicle. Bertone told Rosa to meet him at the garage "quickly" and to bring $1,000.

Rosa complied with this request and rushed over within five minutes. As Rosa drove up with his cousin as backup, he saw Bertone's car leaving the garage being driven by a person who was not Bertone. Rosa chased the car for a while, but it ran red lights and stop signs to get away from the two men. Rosa returned to the garage, and Jordan Jr. denied that Bertone had even been there. Bertone never came home, and his body was never found.[311] Bertone's car was found parked at a local hotel ten days later, but according to police, it contained nothing of interest to the case.

A few weeks later, Bertone's wife was summoned to Porter's house, and he gave her $20,000 from the money that her husband had allegedly stolen from the Jordans. Rosa later testified that Porter wanted to deflect suspicion away from himself and Rosa in Bertone's apparent death. Marvin Droznek, a former mob associate and government witness, also testified that an associate told him after visiting Porter that Bertone would be gone shortly. Apparently, before the purported hit occurred, word was spreading about what would happen. Droznek's testimony seemed to indicate that Porter knew about the hit and may have approved of it.[312]

Muddying the waters even further, Droznek testified that Rosa told him he killed Bertone, and two other mob associates also pointed the finger at Rosa, who had a motive over an alleged $20,000 that Bertone cheated him out of. The prosecution team at the Porter trial discounted that theory based on Rosa's testimony.

Rosa also stated that Chiarelli offered him an Uzi machine gun and a van and indicated that he had provided the same for the Bertone hit when the pair discussed possibly murdering someone else. Chiarelli was charged with providing the murder weapon for the Bertone murder, but he was acquitted of that charge. The prosecution's case for the murder was just too uncertain given the conflicting testimony and the absence of a body.

NOTES

Prologue

1. U.S. Department of Justice, Federal Bureau of Investigation, Pittsburgh Field Office: case name, Mike Genovese; case number, PG 92-235 (Pennsylvania, 1967), FOIPA request no. 1505605-000, 11–17.
2. Ibid., 3–5.
3. John Craig Jr., "Sometimes the Readers Get Restless," *Pittsburgh Post-Gazette*, December 8, 1990, 9.
4. "Gangster-Style Slaying Probed: Penn Hills Man Shot in Westmoreland," *Pittsburgh Press*, December 15, 1967, 23.
5. "Police Probe Slain Man's Last Moves," *Pittsburgh Post-Gazette*, December 16, 1967, 2.
6. Commonwealth of Pennsylvania Crime Commission, "Report on Organized Crime in Pennsylvania," (Conshohocken, PA: 1970), 62.
7. "Pistol Discipline May Be Returning to Rackets World," *Daily Courier*, February 21, 1968, 21.
8. U.S. Department of Justice, Federal Bureau of Investigation, Pittsburgh Field Office: case name, Mike Genovese; case number, PG 92-235 (Pennsylvania, 1967), FOIPA request no. 1505605-000, 3–5.
9. Ibid.
10. Ibid., 11–14.

Chapter 1

11. Commonwealth of Pennsylvania Crime Commission, "Organized Crime in Pennsylvania: A Decade of Change," (Conshohocken, PA: 1990), 117.

12. Richard Gazarik, *Prohibition Pittsburgh* (Charleston: The History Press, 2017), 53.

13. "Racket King Is Slain in Northside Ambush," *Pittsburgh Post-Gazette*, August 7, 1929, 1, 4.

14. "Hunt 'Baby Slayers' in Murder," *Pittsburgh Press*, September 14, 1931, 1–2.

15. "Volpe Aide Murdered," *Pittsburgh Press*, August 11, 1932, 1–2.

16. Torsten Ove, "Mafia Has a Long History Here," *Pittsburgh Post-Gazette*, November 6, 2000, A8–A9.

17. "Reputed Underworld Kingpin: Amato Death Blunts U.S. Braddock Probe," *Pittsburgh Post-Gazette*, February 21, 1973.

18. Matthew Kennedy, "Mob Rule," *Pittsburgh Press*, February 27, 1983, A14; U.S. Department of Justice, Federal Bureau of Investigation, Cincinnati Field Office: case name, La Cosa Nostra; case number, CI 92-557 (Ohio, 1968), 1–4, https://documents.theblackvault.com/documents/jfk/NARA-Oct2017/NARA-Dec15-2017/docid-32305864.pdf.

19. Philip Leonetti, *Mafia Prince* (Philadelphia: Running Press, 2012), 130–35.

20. U.S. Department of Justice, Federal Bureau of Investigation, Pittsburgh Field Office: case name, Mike Genovese; case number, PG 92-235 (Pennsylvania, 1973), FOIPA request no. 1505605-000, 69.

21. Jerry Capeci and Tom Robbins, *Mob Boss: The Life of Little Al D'Arco* (New York: Thomas Dunne Books, 2013), 146–47.

22. U.S. Department of Justice, Federal Bureau of Investigation, Pittsburgh Field Office: case name, Mike Genovese; case number, PG 92-235 (Pennsylvania, 1973), FOIPA request no. 1505605-000, 2, 97.

23. Ibid., 32.

24. Ibid., 1.

25. Torsten Ove, "Michael James Genovese: The Life and Times of the Last Great Pittsburgh Mobster," *Pittsburgh Post-Gazette*, April 19, 2009; U.S. Department of Justice, Federal Bureau of Investigation, Pittsburgh Field Office: case name, Mike Genovese; case number, PG 92-235 (Pennsylvania, 1971), FOIPA request no. 1505605-000, 2–7.

26. U.S. Department of Justice, Federal Bureau of Investigation, Pittsburgh Field Office: case name, Mike Genovese; case number, PG 92-235 (Pennsylvania, 1957), FOIPA request no. 1505605-000, 6–8.

27. Ibid., 12.

28. Torsten Ove, "Government Said Quiet Businessman Was Mafia Boss," *Pittsburgh Post-Gazette*, November 2, 2006, C4.

29. Roger Greenbank, email interview by Paul Hodos, May and June 2022.

30. U.S. Department of Justice, Federal Bureau of Investigation, Pittsburgh Field Office: case name, Mike Genovese; case number, PG 92-235 (Pennsylvania, 1957), FOIPA request no. 1505605-000, 360.

31. Ibid., 1.

32. Ibid., 256.

33. Vince Johnson, "Four Here Linked to Apalachin Case," *Pittsburgh Post-Gazette*, December 4, 1960, 10.

34. "Rifles for Rebels: Gun-Runners, Mob Alliance Probed by U.S.," *Pittsburgh Press*, November 6, 1958, 2.

35. William Deibler, "2-Year Study Shows Power of Racketeers," *Pittsburgh Post-Gazette*, July 3, 1970, 5.

36. Ibid., 74–75; Commonwealth of Pennsylvania Crime Commission, "Organized Crime in Pennsylvania," 114.

37. U.S. Department of Justice, Federal Bureau of Investigation, Pittsburgh Field Office: case name, Mike Genovese; case number, PG 92-235 (Pennsylvania, 1974), FOIPA request no. 1505605-000, 62–96.

38. Ibid., 33.

39. Ibid., 115–18.

40. Ibid., 16.

41. "FBI Probes Youngstown Businessman's Ties to Mafia," *Dayton Daily News*, February 11, 1994, 9.

42. Tim Yovich, "FBI Affidavit Tags Calautti in Laundering," *Youngstown Vindicator*, February 9, 1994, A1.

43. Andrew Sheehan, "Convicted Racketeer to be Crime Boss, Agent Says," *Pittsburgh Post-Gazette*, December 5, 1984.

44. Janet Williams and Robert Johnson, "LaRocca Buried, Media Chased," *Pittsburgh Press*, December 7, 1984, B5; Janet Williams, "Pecora Likely LaRocca Heir," *Pittsburgh Press*, December 5, 1984, B1, B14.

45. "Genovese Now Heads Crime Clan, Panel Says," *Pittsburgh Post-Gazette*, April 27, 1985, 8.

46. IMDB, "Tony Lip: Carmine Lupertazzi, Carmine Lupertazzi Sr.," HBO, *The Sopranos*, https://www.imdb.com/title/tt0141842/characters/nm0513401.

47. Janet Williams, "Panel Says Mob Flourishes by Filling Gambling Void," *Pittsburgh Press*, April 21, 1991, 1.

48. Janet Williams, "Dissension Split Mafia Members, Witness Testifies," *Pittsburgh Press*, September 18, 1990, 9.

49. Janet Williams, "Drug Dealer Testifies He Was Muscled by Mob," *Pittsburgh Press*, September 13, 1990, B1, B4.

50. Commonwealth of Pennsylvania Crime Commission, "Organized Crime in Pennsylvania," 117–18.

51. Janet Williams, "Monroeville Man Accused of Taking Crime Payoffs," *Pittsburgh Press*, April 24, 1990, 9; Torsten Ove, "Obituary: Charles 'Chucky' Porter, Top Mobster and Informant, Dies," *Pittsburgh Post-Gazette*, October 15, 2016, https://www.post-gazette.com/local/east/2016/10/12/Charles-Chucky-Porter-top-mobster-and-informant-has-died/stories/201610120188.

52. Greenbank, email interview, May and June 2022.

53. Torsten Ove, "Agents Ask Judge to Free Ex-Mobster," *Pittsburgh Post-Gazette*, November 30, 2000, A1, A22.

54. Mike Bucsko, "10 Years Can Change a Lot," *Pittsburgh Post-Gazette*, November 30, 2000, 22.

55. Janet Williams, "The Mob on Trial," *Pittsburgh Press*, September 2, 1990, A6.

56. Greenbank, email interview, May and June 2022.

57. Capeci and Robbins, *Mob Boss*, 320.

58. Janet Williams, "Porter Jury Sees Tapes," *Pittsburgh Press*, October 16, 1990, B1, B3; Torsten Ove, "The Stone in the Shoe," *Pittsburgh Post-Gazette*, November 5, 2000, B1–B2.

59. Janet Williams, "Porter Was Big in Pittsburgh Organized Crime, Ex-Mobster Says," *Pittsburgh Press*, October 10, 1990, 15.

60. Greenbank, email interview, May and June 2022.

61. Janet Williams, "Porter Paid by Chinese Gambling Ring, Witness Tells Court," *Pittsburgh Press*, October 12, 1990, B1, B3.

62. "Knifing Follows New Blast in Racket War," *Pittsburgh Press*, January 4, 1958, 1.

63. "Two Held for Court in Burglaries," *Pittsburgh Press*, January 3, 1953, 4.

64. "Woman, 2 Men Held In Baby-Sale Scheme," *Pittsburgh Post-Gazette*, July 30, 1973.

65. Greenbank, email interview, May and June 2022.

66. Commonwealth of Pennsylvania Crime Commission, "Organized Crime in Pennsylvania," 120.

67. Roger Stuart, "La Cosa Nostra Linked to Charitable Bingos Here," *Pittsburgh Press*, February 1, 1992, A1–A3; "Ohio Crime Boss Strollo

Describes His Operations, Political Payoffs," *Pittsburgh Post-Gazette*, March 7, 1999, 14.

68. Mike Bucsko, "Crime Family's Court Sessions in 80s Revealed," *Pittsburgh Post-Gazette*, October 3, 1990, 8.

69. U.S. Department of Justice, Federal Bureau of Investigation, Pittsburgh Field Office: case name, Mike Genovese; case number, PG 92-235 (Pennsylvania, 1985), FOIPA request no. 1505605-000, 41.

70. Kyle Lawson, "Monroeville's Holiday House Offered Memories of Different Time," TribLive, August 14, 2013, https://archive.triblive.com/local/monroeville/monroevilles-holiday-house-offered-memories-of-different-time/#axzz2qmY9p9x3; Greenbank, email interview, May and June 2022.

71. Mike Bucsko, "Crime Trial's Roots Started in East Liberty," *Pittsburgh Post-Gazette*, November 5, 1990, 1, 5.

72. Jason Cato, "Burgh's Mob Ties May Sleep with the Fishes," TribLive, November 4, 2006, https://archive.triblive.com/news/burghs-mob-ties-may-sleep-with-the-fishes/; U.S. Department of Justice, Federal Bureau of Investigation, Pittsburgh Field Office: case name, Mike Genovese; case number, PG 92-235 (Pennsylvania, 1989), FOIPA request no. 1505605-000, 1–4, 24–34.

73. Janet Williams and Roger Stuart, "Mob Prospers Locally, Crime Panel Reports," *Pittsburgh Press*, April 7, 1992, A4.

Chapter 2

74. Paul Maryniak, "Long Arm of Crime: Murder Trial in Cambria Shows Extent of Pittsburgh Underworld's Influence," *Pittsburgh Press*, September 30, 1984, A11.

75. "Charges Filed in Hatchet Murder," *Hanover Evening Sun*, July 20, 1983, 7.

76. "Grand Jury Unveils Altoona Crime Group," *Tyrone Daily Herald*, July 20, 1983, 1.

77. Phil Ray, "Murder Trial: Defense Seeks to Detail 'Family,'" *Altoona Mirror*, March 29, 1985, 13.

78. Paul Maryniak, "Small Altoona Tavern Was Incubator for Plots of Hate and Revenge," *Pittsburgh Press*, December 18, 1983, A14.

79. Paul Maryniak, "Crime Family Thrived in Blair County," *Pittsburgh Press*, December 18, 1983, 1.

80. Maryniak, "Long Arm of Crime," 11.

81. "Burglars Steal Safe," *Altoona Mirror*, May 3, 1957, 1.

82. U.S. Department of Justice, Federal Bureau of Investigation, Pittsburgh Field Office: case name, Mike Genovese; case number, PG 92-235 (Pennsylvania, 1968), FOIPA request no. 1505605-000, 24–25.

83. "News from Around Here," *Tyrone Daily Herald*, August 12, 1983, 1.

84. Ray, "Murder Trial," 13.

85. Maryniak, "Altoona Tavern Was Incubator," A14.

86. Ibid.; Maryniak, "Crime Family Thrived," 1.

87. Maryniak, "Altoona Tavern Was Incubator," A14.

88. Ibid.; Maryniak, "Crime Family Thrived," 1.

89. Commonwealth of Pennsylvania Crime Commission, "Report on Organized Crime," 34.

90. Maryniak, "Long Arm of Crime," 11.

91. Ibid.; Ray, "Murder Trial," 13; Paul, "Altoona Tavern Was Incubator," A14; "Fifth Man Charged in Drug Death," *Indiana Gazette*, July 21, 1983, 29.

92. U.S. Department of Justice, Federal Bureau of Investigation, Pittsburgh Field Office: case name, Mike Genovese; case number, PG 92-235 (Pennsylvania, 1973), FOIPA request no. 1505605-000, 53.

93. "Altoona," *Tyrone Daily Herald*, September 11, 1980, 1.

94. Commonwealth of Pennsylvania Crime Commission, "Organized Crime in Pennsylvania," 79–80.

95. Ibid., 79.

96. "Charges Against 3 Filed," *Latrobe Bulletin*, December 1, 1983, 11.

97. Laurie Fedon, "Grand Jury Indicts State College Man," *Centre Daily Times*, November 30, 1983, 5.

98. Phil Ray, "Caramadre Denies Larocca Link to Altoona Restaurant," *Altoona Mirror*, August 17, 1983, 1.

99. Phil Ray, "McCord Found Guilty of Burning Store," *Altoona Mirror*, December 8, 1986, 9.

100. Maryniak, "Crime Family Thrived," 1; Staff, "Charges Against 3," *Latrobe Bulletin*, 11.

101. "Ebensburg," *Tyrone Daily Herald*, September 24, 1984, 1.

102. "Pair Will Be Tried for Silencing Effort," *Scranton Times-Tribune*, April 6, 1982, 19.

103. "Holidaysburg," *Tyrone Daily Herald*, May 2, 1984, 1.

104. "Ebensburg," *Tyrone Daily Herald*, September 7, 1984, 1; "News from Around Here" *Tyrone Daily Herald*, 1.

105. Paul Maryniak, "Mafia Soldier Gets Life Sentence for Ordering Death of Drug Pusher," *Pittsburgh Press*, October 4, 1984, 15; Maryniak, "Long

Arm of Crime," 11; "Ebensburg," *Tryone Daily Herald*, October 4, 1984, 1; Ray, "Murder Trial," 13.

106. "Opinion: Grand Jury Is Still Necessary," *Altoona Mirror*, September 23, 1988, A4.

107. Paul Maryniak, "Ex-Prosecutor Claims Police, Blair Officials Hurt Probe," *Pittsburgh Press*, August 27, 1985, 6.

108. "In Court," *Altoona Mirror*, August 28, 1988, 10.

109. Michael Race, "Corbo Directs Altoona Crime, Agency Says," *Altoona Mirror*, April 29, 1993, 2.

110. Find A Grave, "Pvt. Alfred F. Corbo," April 21, 2012, https://www.findagrave.com/memorial/89267675/alfred-f-corbo.

Chapter 3

111. U.S. Department of Justice, Federal Bureau of Investigation, Cleveland Field Office: case name, Joseph Naples Jr., et al.; case number, CV 183A-406 (Ohio, 1982), FOIPA request no. 1506135-000, 66.

112. Ibid., 147.

113. U.S. Department of Justice, Federal Bureau of Investigation, Cleveland Field Office: case name, La Cosa Nostra; case number, CV 92-748 (Ohio, 1963), 7–8, https://www.maryferrell.org/showDoc.html?docId=87915#relPageId=2.

114. "Shotgun Blasts End Life of 'Sandy' Naples," *Salem News*, March 12, 1960, 1.

115. "Bomb Shatters Auto, Kills Rackets Figure," *Evening Independent*, July 2, 1962, 1.

116. U.S. Department of Justice, Federal Bureau of Investigation, Cleveland Field Office: case name, Joseph Naples Jr., et al.; case number, CV 183A-406 (Ohio, 1964), FOIPA request no. 1506135-000, 273.

117. Ibid., 273.

118. "Youngstown Bombing Differs from Others," *Salem News*, November 30, 1962, 1.

119. U.S. Department of Justice, Federal Bureau of Investigation, Cleveland Field Office: case name, Joseph Naples Jr., et al.; case number, CV 182-1459 (Ohio, 1963), FOIPA request no. 1506135-000, 83–84.

120. Ibid., 133, 135.

121. William Kazziah, "Naples Charged in Slaying," *Akron Beacon Journal*, March 6, 1975.

122. John Dunphy, "Victim Recounts Shooting," *Akron Beacon Journal*, January 29, 1976, A1, A18.

123. Timothy Yovich, "FBI Affidavit Ties Naples to 2 Killings, Car Arson," *Youngstown Vindicator*, June 27, 1983.

124. "Cleveland-Pittsburgh Rivalry: A Deadly Game," *Youngstown Vindicator*, July 18, 1982, A9.

125. "Important Crime Case Prosecution to Begin," *Bucyrus Telegraph-Forum*, March 30, 1978, 14.

126. Peter Phipps, "Mahoning Sheriff at OK Corral," *Akron Beacon Journal*, October 10, 1982, A1–A8.

127. "Sheriff Tells Jury FBI Ruined Plan to Break Mob," *Akron Beacon Journal*, April 29, 1983, B4.

128. "Jury Decides Sheriff Innocent of All Counts," *Lancaster Eagle-Gazette*, June 17, 1983, 5.

129. Elena Schneider, "James A. Traficant Jr., Cast Out by Congress in Bribery Case, Dies at 73," *New York Times*, September 27, 2014, https://www.nytimes.com/2014/09/28/us/politics/james-a-traficant-jr-who-was-expelled-from-congress-after-bribery-conviction-dies-at-73.html.

130. Kenneth J. Evans, "Mob Here Taking Over Youngstown," *Pittsburgh Post-Gazette*, July 17, 1982, 1, 4.

131. Bob Jackson, "Man Pleads Innocent in 21-Year-Old Murder Case," *Youngstown Vindicator*, June 8, 2002, https://vindyarchives.com/news/2002/jun/08/man-pleads-innocent-in-21-year-old-murder-case/; "On This Date In," *Vindicator*, January 15, 2004, https://vindyarchives.com/news/2004/jan/15/today-is-monday-jan-12-the-12th-day-of-2004/.

132. "Death Ruled a Homicide," *Akron Beacon Journal*, April 13, 1979, A7.

133. "Suit Filed by Widow for Data on Insurance," *Telegraph-Forum*, July 10, 1981, 7.

134. J.R. Freeman, "State's Crime Families Becoming Stronger," *Lebanon Daily News*, February 24, 1983, 4.

135. Dennis Mangan, "Years Ago February 14th," 21WFMJ, February 13, 2020, https://www.wfmj.com/story/41697996/years-ago-or-february-14th.

136. "Prosecutors Try to Finger Hitman with His Grand Jury Testimony," *Marysville Journal-Tribune*, April 14, 1983, 8.

137. "Police Believe Killing a Mistake," *Mansfield News-Journal*, February 27, 1981, 9.

138. "Crime War Tie Probed in Peninsula Car Blast," *Akron Beacon Journal*, April 21, 1981, C1.

139. "FBI Alleged Mafia 'War,'" *Sentinel*, July 16, 1982, 4.

140. "Tip from Theft Ring Investigation Solves 1981 Organized Crime Slaying," *Chillicothe Gazette*, February 24, 2002, 3.

141. Bill Moushey, "Mafia Boss Sheds Light on Crime Here," *Pittsburgh Post-Gazette*, December 23, 1985, 1.

142. "Ohio Crime Boss Strollo," *Pittsburgh Post-Gazette*, A14.

143. "Youngstown Mobster Facing Weapons Charge," *Bucyrus Telegraph-Forum*, October 11, 1983, 3.

144. U.S. Department of Justice, Federal Bureau of Investigation, Cleveland Field Office: case name, Joseph Naples Jr., et al.; case number, CV 183A-406 (Ohio, 1982), FOIPA request no. 1506135-000, 6–116.

145. "Mahoning Sheriff Expects Organized Crime Charge," *Marion Star*, March 31, 1982, 2; "Vincenzo 'Jimmy' Prato; Owned Calla Mar Manor," *Youngstown Vindicator*, October 17, 1988, 2.

146. Commonwealth of Pennsylvania Crime Commission, "Organized Crime in Pennsylvania," 125.

147. Ibid., 116.

Chapter 4

148. Ray Formanek, "Bar Owner Says Hankish Helped Arrange Killing," *Pittsburgh Post-Gazette*, July 18, 1990, 41.

149. Jim Memmott, "For Voting in Rochester, Mob Kingpin Frank Valenti Got Three Years in Pittsburgh," *Democrat & Chronicle*, February 18, 2019, https://www.democratandchronicle.com/story/news/2019/02/18/remarkable-rochester-mobster-frank-valenti-jake-russo-pittsburg-voter-fraud/2904628002/.

150. Taylor Lynda Guydon, "Witness Says He Was a Paid Killer for Hankish," *Pittsburgh Post-Gazette*, July 20, 1990, 6.

151. Shane Hoover and Tim Botos, "The Madam Must Die," *Canton Rep*, October 20, 2019, https://www.cantonrep.com/story/news/local/canton/2019/10/20/the-madam-must-die/2486760007/.

152. George Sidiropolis, *Murder Never Dies: Crime and Corruption in the Friendly City* (Terra Alta, WV: Headline Books Inc., 2017), chapter 44.

153. "Burglary Verdict Upheld by Court," *Raleigh Register*, June 19, 1962, 1.

154. "Parole Granted Wheeling Man," *Weirton Daily Times*, June 26, 1963, 20.

155. "FBI Enters Wheeling Blast Case," *Weirton Daily Times*, January 18, 1964, 1, https://www.newspapers.com/clip/93865075/hanksih-car-bomb-details/.

156. Bob Powell, "July 14, 1900: Gangster 'Big Bill' Lias Possibly Born in Wheeling," West Virginia Public Broadcasting, July 14, 2017, https://www.wvpublic.org/radio/2017-07-14/july-14-1900-gangster-big-bill-lias-possibly-born-in-wheeling.

157. "Attorney Says Chief Issued Misinformation," *Raleigh Register*, January 24, 1964, 2; "Police Study Wreckage of Hankish Auto," *Weirton Daily Times*, January 20, 1964, 1; "Car Bombed: Ex-Con Hurt in Gangland Style Blast," *Charleston Daily Mail*, January 17, 1964, 1; "Hankish Given 50-50 Chance," *Beckley Post-Herald*, January 19, 1964, 2.

158. Roger Stuart, "Killed for Hankish, Trial Witness Says," *Pittsburgh Press*, July 19, 1990, 1.

159. "Hankish Took Bets of High Rollers Like Art Rooney Sr., U.S. Says," *Pittsburgh Press*, July 18, 1990, 1, A3.

160. Jan Ackerman, "W. Va. Jury to Hear 26-Year Tale of Racketeering," *Pittsburgh Post-Gazette*, June 23, 1990, 4.

161. "14 Arraigned on Car Charges," *Weirton Daily Times*, May 27, 1969, 17.

162. "Jury Finds Hankish Guilty of Firebombing," *Raleigh Register*, July 27, 1973, 12.

163. Maryniak, "Crime Family Thrived," 1.

164. Commonwealth of Pennsylvania Crime Commission, "Organized Crime in Pennsylvania," 121.

165. Greenbank, email interview, May and June 2022.

166. Janet Williams, "District's La Cosa Nostra Is Strongest in State," *Pittsburgh Press*, April 14, 1991, B7.

167. U.S. Department of Justice, Federal Bureau of Investigation, Cleveland Field Office: case name, Joseph Naples Jr.; case number, CV 183A-634 (Ohio, 1982), FOIPA request no. 1506135-000, 9–29.

168. Roger Stuart, "Hankish Enters Guilty Plea to 9 Counts; Others Dropped," *Pittsburgh Press*, July 24, 1990, 1.

169. "Hankish Took Bets," *Pittsburgh Press*, 1, A3.

170. Roger Stuart, "Smuggler Says Hankish Used Mob Influence to Cancel Hit," *Pittsburgh Press*, July 20, 1990, 11.

171. Ray, "Owner Says Hankish Helped," 41.

172. "Fayette Man's Slayer Hunted," *Pittsburgh Press*, April 21, 1978, A10.

173. Harry Tkach, "Mannarino Crime Family Tied to Suspect in Contract Killing," *Pittsburgh Post-Gazette*, July 10, 1981, 1, 3.

174. Janet Williams, "Organized Crime Trial Gives Public Look at the Mob," *Pittsburgh Press*, September 10, 1990, D1.

175. Bill Heltzel, "Obituary: Robert Bricker/One of Region's Most Notorious Killers," *Pittsburgh Post-Gazette*, June 25, 2000, https://old.post-gazette.com/obituaries/20000625bricker4.asp.

176. "Man's Slayer Hunted," *Pittsburgh Press*, A10.

177. "Porter Disputes Witnesses' Testimony That Links Him to Criminal Activities," *Pittsburgh Press*, October 18, 1990, B5.

178. *Encyclopaedia Britannica*, "Economy of West Virginia," https://www.britannica.com/place/West-Virginia/Economy.

179. Tom Searls, "Preparing for Accused Mobster Trial, Guilty Pleas are Taken," *Tyrone Daily Herald*, June 25, 1990, 2.

180. Roger Stuart, "Mrs. Hankish: Crime Partner or Prisoner?" *Pittsburgh Press*, July 24, 1990, 1.

181. Carmen Lee, "11 Indicted for Rackets Centered in Wheeling," *Pittsburgh Post-Gazette*, October 3, 1989, 8.

182. "Gambling Operation Raided," *Hazleton Standard-Speaker*, December 21, 1987, 9.

183. Lee, "11 Indicted," 8.

184. Roger Stuart, "Smuggler Says Hankish Used Mob Influence to Cancel Hit," *Pittsburgh Press*, July 20, 1990, 11.

185. Jan Ackerman, "Crime Boss Sentenced to 33 and a Half Years," *Pittsburgh Post-Gazette*, October 26, 1990, 6.

186. Jan Ackerman, "Hankish Pleads Guilty, Freeing Wife of Charges," *Pittsburgh Post-Gazette*, July 25, 1990, 1, 6.

187. Jason Cato, "Son of W.Va. Gambling Kingpin Pleads Guilty," TribLive, January 25, 2007, https://archive.triblive.com/news/son-of-w-va-gambling-kingpin-pleads-guilty/.

Chapter 5

188. Mike Bucsko, "9 Crime Figures Found Guilty," *Pittsburgh Post-Gazette*, October 30, 1990, 1; John, "Readers Get Restless," 9.

189. U.S. Department of Justice, Federal Bureau of Investigation, Pittsburgh Field Office: case name, Mike Genovese; case number, PG 92-235 (Pennsylvania, 1969), FOIPA request no. 1505605-000, 27.

190. "Suspect in One Case Convicted in Another," *Pittsburgh Press*, May 22, 1981, 2; Harry Tkach and Fritz Huysman, "Man at Trial Seized, Tied to Big 'Grass' Haul," *Pittsburgh Post-Gazette*, May 15, 1981, 4.

191. Commonwealth of Pennsylvania Crime Commission, "Organized Crime in Pennsylvania," 127.

192. Harry Tkach, "Tale of Threat Fails to Alter Bond Setting," *Pittsburgh Post-Gazette*, November 11, 1982, 7.

193. Janet Williams, "Prosdocimo Chose Crime at Early Age," *Pittsburgh Press*, September 10, 1990, D1.

194. Mike Bucsko, "Details Given on Racket Killings," *Pittsburgh Post-Gazette*, September 12, 1990, 8.

195. Janet Williams, "Prosdocimo Says He Bribed Judge, Hit City Councilman," *Pittsburgh Press*, September 12, 1990, B1.

196. Mike Bucsko, "Rackets Trial Spiced with Names of Officials," *Pittsburgh Post-Gazette*, September 13, 1990, 6.

197. Charles Lynch, "Case of Monessen Man Slain in Parking Lot Is Puzzling," *Pittsburgh Post-Gazette*, June 18, 1979, 10.

198. Tkach, "Crime Family Tied to Suspect," 1, 3.

199. Paul Ayars, "Gunshot Victim Knew Killer, Police Believe," *Pittsburgh Post-Gazette*, September 26, 1979, 1.

200. Jim Cuddy Jr., "Arrests Introduce Public to Suspects Police Know Well," *Pittsburgh Press*, April 20, 1990, B1, B4; Paul Maryniak, "It's Payback Time, Ex-Pitt Player Says in Drug-Slay Trial," *Pittsburgh Press*, November 13, 1981, A12; Harry Tkach, "Gangbusters," *Pittsburgh Post-Gazette*, June 11, 1981, 1, 4.

201. Susan Mannella, "Jury Rules Third-Degree Murder in 'Hit' Trial," *Pittsburgh Post-Gazette*, October 22, 1982, 36.

202. "Backyard Boxers," *Pittsburgh Press*, April 5, 1953, 34.

203. Janet Williams, "High Life," *Pittsburgh Press*, September 28, 1986, B1, B7.

204. Commonwealth of Pennsylvania Crime Commission, "Organized Crime in Pennsylvania," 127.

205. David Guo, "Mazzei Heroin-Dealing Case Goes to Jury," *Pittsburgh Post-Gazette*, March 12, 1981, 5.

206. Toni Locy, "5 Convictions in Drug Case Called Big Step in Crackdown," *Pittsburgh Press*, March 14, 1985, S6.

207. U.S. Department of Justice, Federal Bureau of Investigation, Pittsburgh Field Office: case name, Eugene Gesuale; case number, PG 179A-133 (Pennsylvania, 1981), FOIPA request no. 1505996-000, 7.

208. Torsten, "Stone in the Shoe," B1, B2.

209. Jason Cato, "Pittsburgh Mobster 'Nick the Blade' Dies in Florida," TribLive, August 3, 2016, https://archive.triblive.com/news/pittsburgh-mobster-nick-the-blade-dies-in-florida/.

210. Janet Williams, "Drug Suspect's Life of Luxury Detailed by FBI at Bond Hearing," *Pittsburgh Press*, July 19, 1986, C3.

211. Bohdan Hodiak, "Witness: Gesuale Got Gems for Drug," *Pittsburgh Post-Gazette*, September 18, 1986, 3.

212. Janet Williams, "Ex-FBI Worker Tells of Leaks to Mob," *Pittsburgh Press*, October 5, 1990, D7.

213. Joyce McDonald, ed., "'The Blade' Nabbed in Jamaica," *Pentacle* 7, no. 1 (January 1987): 28, https://www.ojp.gov/pdffiles1/Digitization/105970NCJRS.pdf.

214. Jason Cato, "'Nick the Blade' Dies."

215. Mike Bucsko, "'Family' Adopted New Member," *Pittsburgh Post-Gazette*, September 14, 1990, 6.

216. Janet Williams, "Indictments Strike at Heart of Mob," *Pittsburgh Press*, April 20, 1990, B1, B4; Williams Janet, "Dissension Split Mafia Members, Witness Testifies," *Pittsburgh Press*, September 18, 1990, B1, B5.

217. Jim Cuddy Jr., "Ex-Assistant DA Arrested in Court, Charged with Aiding Cocaine Sellers," *Pittsburgh Press*, April 13, 1988, A1, A5.

218. Jim Cuddy Jr., "Drug Investigations Spotlight Mysteries of Monroeville Man," *Pittsburgh Press*, August 2, 1987, A11–A12.

219. Stuart, "La Cosa Nostra Linked," A1, A3.

220. Janet Williams, "Porter OK'd Beating, Jury Told," *Pittsburgh Press*, September 26, 1990, C1, C7.

221. Mike Bucsko, "Suspects Knew of Probe, FBI Says," *Pittsburgh Post-Gazette*, October 16, 1990, 5.

222. Williams, "Mob on Trial," A6.

223. Mike Bucsko, "U.S. Reduces Key Witness' Prison Term," *Pittsburgh Post-Gazette*, January 19, 1991, 9.

224. Mike Bucsko, "2 Sent to Prison in Mobster Trials," *Pittsburgh Post-Gazette*, January 23, 1991, 9.

Chapter 6

225. Ove, "Stone in the Shoe," B2.

226. "Cop's Stamp Role Aired in U.S. Trial," *Pittsburgh Post-Gazette*, January 19, 1972, 20.

227. U.S. Department of Justice, Federal Bureau of Investigation, Pittsburgh Field Office: case name, Mike Genovese; case number, PG 92-235 (Pennsylvania, 1985), FOIPA request no. 1505605-000, 41.

228. Commonwealth of Pennsylvania Crime Commission, "Organized Crime in Pennsylvania," 118; U.S. Department of Justice, Federal Bureau of Investigation, Pittsburgh Field Office: case name, Henry A. Zottola, also known as "Zebo"; case number, 281A-PG-61412 (Pennsylvania, 1995), FOIPA request no. 1505861-000.

229. Marylynne Pitz, "Conley's Poker Empire Survived Three Raids," *Pittsburgh Post-Gazette*, April 19, 1997, A7.

230. Marylynne Pitz, "5 Charged in Casino Laundering Scheme," *Pittsburgh Post-Gazette*, April 19, 1997, A1, A7.

231. Bill Heltzel, "Guilty Plea to Federal Charges," *Pittsburgh Post-Gazette*, April 14, 1998, 12.

232. Tony Perry, "17 Indicted in Indian Casino Probe," *Los Angeles Times*, April 19, 1997, A22.

233. Bill Heltzel, "Local Organized Crime Figure Recently Sentenced," *Pittsburgh Post-Gazette*, August 22, 1998, 10.

Chapter 7

234. Patricia Meade, "Testimony Details Bribery, Killings," *Vindicator*, March 4, 1999, A1–A5.

235. "Reputed Mob Figure Shot to Death in Ohio," *Pittsburgh Press*, August 20, 1991, 11; Bill Moushey, "Ohio Mobster with Ties Here Is Shot to Death," *Pittsburgh Post-Gazette*, August 21, 1991, 5.

236. "Reputed Killing of Mobster May Spark Some Retaliations," *Tribune*, August 21, 1991, 13.

237. Mark Niquette and Bertram de Souza, "Bushwhacker Shoots Racketeer to Death," *Vindicator*, August 20, 1991, 1.

238. "Ohio Gambling Facility Run by District Mob," *Pittsburgh Press*, April 6, 1987, B5.

239. "Deputy, Ex-Chief Are Indicted in Mahoning," *Telegraph-Forum*, April 22, 1988, 2.

240. Mike Tobin, "End of the Line," *Cleveland Scene*, April 8, 1999, https://www.clevescene.com/cleveland/end-of-the-line/Content?oid=1472059.

241. "Ohio Crime Boss Strollo," *Pittsburgh Post-Gazette*, 14.

242. "Strollo Denies Passing Money," *Lancaster Eagle-Gazette*, July 16, 1963, 11.

243. Ibid.; Greenbank, email interview, May and June 2022.

244. Commonwealth of Pennsylvania Crime Commission, "Organized Crime in Pennsylvania," 118.

245. Marylynne Pitz, "North Hills Lawyer Admits Fronting Mob's Casino Deal," *Pittsburgh Post-Gazette*, June 21, 1997, 10.

246. "Bank Theft Family Affair for Buckeyes," *Dayton Daily News*, June 2, 1992, 8.

247. Bill Heltzel, "Mob Rule in Youngstown," *Pittsburgh Post-Gazette*, December 7, 1997, C8.

248. Vince Guerrieri, "On the 40th Anniversary of Youngstown's "Black Monday, An Oral History," *Belt Magazine*, September 19, 2017, https://beltmag.com/40th-anniversary-youngstowns-black-monday-oral-history/.

249. FindLaw, "*United States v. Riddle*, 99-3405 (6th Cir. 2001)," https://caselaw.findlaw.com/us-6th-circuit/1236282.html.

250. "3 Charged in 94 Theft at Museum in Lexington," *Paducah Sun*, September 19, 1999, 5.

251. "Three 'Mafia Wannabees' Indicted in Museum Heist," *Owensboro Messenger-Inquirer*, June 10, 2000, 6.

252. Lisa Cornwell, "Racketeering, Gambling Charges Leveled," *Marysville Journal-Tribune*, December 12, 1997.

253. M.R. Kropko, "Prosecutor Admits Taking Mob Bribes," *Daily Kent Stater*, September 22, 1999, https://dks.library.kent.edu/?a=d&d=dks19990922-01.2.11&e=-------en-20--1--txt-txIN-------.

254. Mark Niquette, "Owner of B.J. Alan Denies Deal with Gotti," *Vindicator*, March 4, 1999, A3.

255. Meade, "Testimony Details," A1–A5.

256. "Traficant Aide Met Mobsters," *Dayton Daily News*, May 11, 1997, 24.

257. Meade, "Testimony Details," A1–A5.

258. David Grann, "Crimetown USA: The City That Fell in Love with the Mob," *New Republic*, July 10, 2000, https://newrepublic.com/article/68973/crimetown-usa.

259. "Suspected Crime Figure Killed," *Pittsburgh Post-Gazette*, June 5, 1996, 37.

260. "Investigate Killing," *Bryan Times*, October 27, 1997.

261. Marc Smerling, "Pull the Trigger and You're In," *Marc Smerling's Crooked City Podcast*, interview with Mark Batcho, August 17, 2022.

262. Heltzel, "Crimetown USA"; "Ex-Prosecutor Shot in Leg," *Mansfield News Journal*, April 2, 1996, 13.

263. Glaberson William, "Mob Figure Admits Roles in Murders, Including Judge's," *New York Times*, August 14, 2004, https://www.nytimes.com/2004/08/14/nyregion/mob-figure-admits-roles-in-murders-including-judge-s.html.

264. Guo, "Figure Recently Sentenced," 10.

265. Bertram de Souza, "The Mafia in Youngstown—The Hit on Paul Gains, Part 2," *Bertram de Souza's Scribbler Podcast*, interview with Paul Gains, August 26, 2020, www.youtube.com.

266. "Trial Witness Gets Dead Bird in the Mail," *Marysville Journal-Tribune*, December 3, 1998, 1.

267. "Three Alleged Mobsters Await Verdict of Illegal Gambling," *Bucyrus Telegraph-Forum*, March 12, 1999, 2.

268. Andrew Welsh-Huggins, "Trial May Split Open Youngstown Mob," *Mansfield News-Journal*, November 29, 1998.

269. de Souza, "Mafia in Youngstown."

270. TribLive, "Former Pittsburgh Mobster, Youngstown Mob Boss Lenny Strollo Dies at Age 90," May 20, 2021, https://triblive.com/local/regional/former-pittsburgh-mobster-youngstown-mob-boss-lenny-strollo-dies-at-age-90/.

Chapter 8

271. Ove, "Agents Ask Judge," A1, A22.

272. "More Mafia Suspects Hunted," *Latrobe Bulletin*, July 24, 1969, 17.

273. Janet Williams, "Administrator Charges Teamsters Are Trying to Thwart His Efforts," *Pittsburgh Press*, November 19, 1989, B8; McKay Jim, "Drivers Support Teamsters Leader," *Pittsburgh Post-Gazette*, August 3, 1990, 15, 16.

274. Janet Williams, "Cozza Will Have Chance to Respond in Teamster Case," *Pittsburgh Press*, July 26, 1990, B1, B4; Janet Williams, "Cozza Crime Figure Ties Defended by Attorney," *Pittsburgh Press*, August 3, 1990, B1.

275. Jim McKay and Ernie Hoffman, "Ruled Newspaper Teamsters Union in City for 41 Years," *Pittsburgh Post-Gazette*, December 11, 1996, C13.

276. Bill Moushey and Jim McKay, "U.S. Trying to Oust Union's Leaders," *Pittsburgh Post-Gazette*, March 29, 2000, B1, B2.

277. Jim McKay, "Oversight Ordered for Local Union," *Pittsburgh Post-Gazette*, March 14, 2001, B1, B8.

278. Torsten Ove, "Leader of Laborers Union, Champion Boxer," *Pittsburgh Post-Gazette*, December 27, 2010, B1–B2.

279. James Rodgers, "Operated Only Dice, Cards, Ciancutti Says," *Pittsburgh Press*, February 26, 1963, 2.

280. Torsten Ove, "Frank D. Amato Jr. Although Identified as Mafia Figure, He Was Never Charged with Crime," *Pittsburgh Post-Gazette*, November 7, 2003, B19.

281. "Gambling Raid Nets Kingpin, 14 Others," *Pittsburgh Post-Gazette*, October 24, 2000, B1, B2.

282. Greenbank, email interview, May and June 2022; Jason Vest and Ken Silverstein, "Trump's Gamble for Indian Wampum," *Village Voice*, July 14, 2020, https://www.villagevoice.com/2020/07/14/trumps-gamble-for-indian-wampum-2/; Donald Mitchell, *Wampum* (New York: Overlook Press, 2016), 273.

283. Matthew Junker, "Tapes Hint to Violent Nature of Crime Ring," TribLive, January 23, 2001, https://archive.triblive.com/news/tapes-hint-to-violent-nature-of-crime-ring/.

284. "Raid Nets Kingpin," *Pittsburgh Post-Gazette*, B1, B2.

285. "Alleged Gambling Organizer Sentenced," *Indiana Gazette*, March 6, 2002, 3.

286. Torsten Ove, "North Huntingdon Drug Lord Cuts Deal, Gets Prison," *Pittsburgh Post-Gazette*, February 10, 2004, https://www.post-gazette.com/local/westmoreland/2004/02/10/North-Huntingdon-drug-lord-cuts-deal-gets-prison/stories/200402100137.

287. Rich Cholodofsky, "Head of Pittsburgh Area Gambling Ring, Son, Plead Guilty to Running Numbers" TribLive, September 16, 2020, https://triblive.com/local/westmoreland/head-of-pittsburgh-area-gambling-ring-son-plead-guilty-to-running-numbers/.

288. Bucsko, "10 Years," A1, A22.

289. Ove, "Obituary: Charles 'Chucky' Porter."

290. Greenbank, email interview, May and June 2022.

291. Ove, "Stone in the Shoe," B1.

292. Ove, "Quiet Businessman," C4.

Chapter 9

293. Michael Fuoco, "Purolator Robbery in 1982 Remains Unsolved," *Pittsburgh Post-Gazette*, March 2, 2012, A1, A7.

294. Greenbank, email interview, May and June 2022.

295. Robert Baird, "Man Gets 5 Years in Stolen Rifle Sale," *Pittsburgh Press*, August 3, 1989, B5.

296. Torsten Ove, "Obituary: Geno Chiarelli/Powerful Figure in Pittsburgh Mafia," *Pittsburgh Post-Gazette*, June 21, 2012, https://www.post-gazette.com/news/obituaries/2012/06/21/Obituary-Geno-Chiarelli-Powerful-figure-in-Pittsburgh-Mafia/stories/201206210241

297. Mike Bucsko, "St. Pat's Day Robbery Still Stumps Officials," *Pittsburgh Post-Gazette*, March 16, 1998, A17.

298. Roger Stuart and Don Hopey, "Bookie's Death Investigated for Rackets Link," *Pittsburgh Press*, October 26, 1988, 1, 4.

299. Ibid.

300. Mary Stolberg, "Jimmy Goodnight's Murder Baffles the Rocks," *Pittsburgh Press*, March 25, 1979, B1.

301. Lisa Mullen, "The Murder and Mayhem of Pittsburgh's Historic Mafia," *Gazette 2.0*, April 14, 2021, https://www.gazette20.com/post/the-murder-and-mayhem-of-pittsburgh-s-historic-mafia; "McKees Rocks Ex-Officer Found Strangled on Street," *Pittsburgh Post-Gazette*, August 1, 1987, 9B; Roger Stuart and Don Hopey, "Gambling Way of Life Turns Deadly in McKees Rocks," *Pittsburgh Press*, October 30, 1988, 1.

302. Paula Reed Ward, "Skosnik Charged with Bribery, Case-Fixing, Abuses of Power," *Pittsburgh Post-Gazette*, November 22, 2005, 1, 8.

303. Ibid.

304. Stuart and Hopey, "Bookie's Death Investigated," 1, 4.

305. Brian Lowry, "TV Review: A&E's *Godfather of Pittsburgh*," *Variety*, November 7, 2014, https://variety.com/2014/tv/reviews/tv-review-godfather-of-pittsburgh-1201347522/.

306. Kari Andren, "Hill District Native Williams Convicted in Numbers Racket Remembered as Loving Dad, Grandfather," TribLive, April 2, 2016, https://archive.triblive.com/local/pittsburgh-allegheny/hill-district-native-williams-convicted-in-numbers-racket-remembered-as-loving-dad-grandfather/.

307. Douglas Root, "Authorities Sift for Clues in Blast at Joey's," *Pittsburgh Press*, January 16, 1982, 2.

308. Bill Moushey, "Bertone Disappearance a Traceless Mystery," *Pittsburgh Post-Gazette*, July 29, 1985, 1.

309. Jim Gallagher, "Bertone Allowed to Manage Restaurant," *Pittsburgh Post-Gazette*, June 3, 1982, 4.

310. Mike Bucsko, "Protected Witness Implicates 8 of 9 Defendants," *Pittsburgh Post-Gazette*, September 18, 1990, 6.

311. Cristina Rouvalis, "Joseph Bertone Is Missing," *Pittsburgh Post-Gazette*, June 25, 1985, 5.

312. Mike Bucsko, "Bertone Mystery Pervades Testimony in Racketeering Trial," *Pittsburgh Post-Gazette*, October 10, 1990, 5.

ABOUT THE AUTHOR

Paul N. Hodos is a two-time book author, article author and former FBI supervisory intelligence analyst. He received his undergraduate degree in history at Saint Vincent College in Latrobe, Pennsylvania, and his graduate degree in strategic intelligence at the National Intelligence University in Bethesda, Maryland. Paul was born in Johnstown, Pennsylvania, and raised in Johnstown; Oakland, Maryland; and Ligonier, Pennsylvania. He currently resides in Kensington, Maryland, with his very supportive wife and kids.